Son of a Red Devil

T0319191

Lukemba Gelindo

Langaa Research & Publishing CIG
Mankon, Bamenda

Publisher
Langaa RPCIG
Langaa Research & Publishing Common Initiative Group
P.O. Box 902 Mankon
Bamenda
North West Region
Cameroon
Langaagrp@gmail.com
www.langaa-rpcig.net

Distributed in and outside N. America by African Books Collective
orders@africanbookscollective.com
www.africanbookcollective.com

ISBN: 9956-728-16-0

Son of a Red Devil

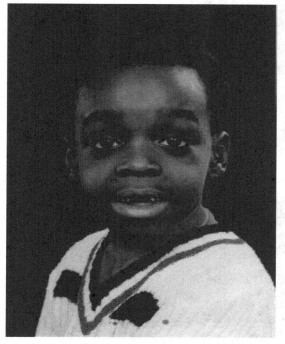

GUST-STAF HELLEMANS

"VOETBALLERS HEBBEN
GEEN RESPECT
MEER VOOR MEKAAR"

Introduction

This memoir is about me. I was adopted by a former football player and captain, August Hellemans - also called Gustaf - of the national Belgian team, The Red Devils. My brother and I were adopted after we were abandoned in a nursery home where we were mistreated. I grew up in a Flemish village where people had never before seen a black person. In general, Flemings are still surprised when they hear blacks speaking their language fluently. This can lead to boring situations during, for example, a job interview where I had to explain over and over again as to how I learned it.

Further, my memoir is about the differences in mentality between the Flemings and Walloons viewed from a black perspective and through the eyes of someone who is intimately familiar with both cultures. My parents were Flemings but I always went to French-speaking schools. Among other things, it is also my aim to denounce how young black children get objectified by the rich and famous as the latest 'must have' things, designer accessories up for adoption. Like in the rest of the world, this trend is taken by people from all walk of lives. The whole thing is written in a self-loathing way and I always try to be as politically correct as possible (my arse).

Lukemba Gelindo
Rue de l'Orphelinat 30A bt 78
1070 Bruxelles (Belgium)
Tel: 0032. 486.557.109
lukembagelindo@gmail.com

Chapter 1

What's behind me, is my arse
Great Flemish poet and politician
Bart De Wever

I was sitting in the car with these three women: my adoptive mother, a friend of hers called Lucienne and her daughter Kathleen. While I was lying with my head on Kathleen's lap, I could barely stand the smell coming from her crotch area. We were all heading to a town the exact name of which I will never bring myself to reveal. Should this town ever gain some recognition through my writing, I can only say that that was not my intention. It does not deserve the slightest publicity; rather, it should forever remain in oblivion. However, I am aware that it would not be that difficult to locate. For now, let me just say I am talking about a region that is home to a species of human being with whom I have never felt comfortable or really liked: the Flemings.

I had been in a hospital for a throat operation in Duffel, a region of Antwerp. My parents had been taking turns staying over at night so I would not feel lonely. On my last day in the hospital, my mother had been proudly showing me around the hospital ward. However, a certain nurse must have taken offence at such scenes of tenderness. I could see her going into a drawer, and as I rightly guessed, she brought out a suppository. I hated it! Normally, she was not the one who administered them to me. I guess she also wanted to take part in the action and have a souvenir of her own. After all, it might take some time before she saw a black arse again. I cried, fidgeted, and tried to block her with my hands, but she persistently slapped them away with her fists, right in front of my parents. It offended them, but they thought it best to sit there and do nothing. Anyway, it was over now.

I had been adopted, but somehow I never bore my adoptive father's name. I think my parents hesitated to go all the way with the adoption procedures because of a concern that my biological parents might crop up and try to contact me. It took decades before I got any sign of my siblings again. Originally, my older Bruno and I were abandoned at a nursery. Actually I do not think that the right word is "abandoned," we were just never reclaimed. As far as my early beginnings go, that is as much as I know. I never knew how on earth my older Bruno and I ended up in a nursery in a god-forsaken town called Brussegem in Flanders. The Flemish sounding name of this town must have been an omen of things to come.

Apparently, the woman in charge at the nursery we called "mami" had mistreated us; our mistreatment eventually became public and turned out to be a major case of child abuse. I said 'apparently' because, thankfully, I do not have any recollections of this alleged wrongdoing. My memories of that period are just too vague. When I got a bit older my parents told me that I had been severely malnourished and that they were not allowed to feed me in the beginning just like any other kid. I do remember going to school there with Bruno, holding hands and other things; but that's just about it. I must have been three or four years old at most. Whenever she came home, Kathleen, who worked there as a caretaker at the nursery, would always complain and cry about the way we were treated. This time however, my future dad happened to be around. He was a close family friend and was carrying out some repair work. He was very moved by what she told him and told her that he would see what he could about it. At first we were invited to come along for a weekend; then we were invited again and again thereafter. Eventually, after some administrative wriggling, they obtained the right to keep us as theirs permanently.

After our time in the nursery, Bruno and I went to a boarding school somewhere in Dilbeek (Brussels), then later to a care home for children in Oudergem. It was called Home Empain. The name was derived from the name of the Baron-Empain, a rich Belgian businessman. He had been kidnapped in Paris and held hostage for ransom for more than two months. It was one of the biggest criminal cases in the seventies. Even though I spent a great deal of my life in this town, I did not attend school there due to the intervention of a renowned francophone judge for youth protection in Belgium, Miss Marie Dumont-Baguette. She was the one who granted my parents custody over us, but on one condition: we had to go to a French-speaking school instead of a Flemish one. Maybe she did not want to see us turn into two little freaks with only the Flemish language, or more precisely its dialect, with which to express ourselves, or to be too alienated from the Congolese diaspora. However, with this decision, this woman saved my life! After all, I am talking about the seventies.

Flemings, especially those living outside urban areas, had basically never seen a Negro at the time, at least not up close. They came from all over town to visit us at my parents' home, just as people do when they go to the circus. All the while I lived there, they never really bothered to stop pointing fingers, gawp at me, or use me as a nice source of inspiration to rekindle any flagging conversation. I know for sure that had this town or region been French speaking, I would never have experienced half of what I had to go through. This is quite odd because I am talking about a Flemish town that is separated by only twenty minutes from Brussels. It is easy to reach as it is situated on a motorway. Using this motorway on my way back to Brussels, I always had the feeling of going back through centuries as I passed these 'communes à facilité' - towns that have Flemish as the official language but include Francophone areas as well. Basically what I mean is, the nearer I got to French-speaking areas, the more I felt part of civilisation again.

People from outside Belgium might wonder what it is that sets these two ethnically and culturally distinct tribes so far apart, despite the fact they live next to each other. Just to say that it would be a question of mentality would sound a bit too simplistic. But what I do know is that in order to have a better understanding of what characterizes the Fleming, it is imperative to go back to his peasant roots because that is what he is and basically always has been: a peasant. It is something he is damn well aware of and it is lack of any cultural references worth to speak of and inferiority complex that sometimes fills him with so much hatred towards the Walloon. It is hard to find a Walloon who can name one famous Flemish song, writer, or whatever that can be related to Flemish culture. There is simply no interest in it but rather disdain, utter indifference mixed with shame for everything this language represents. I have never felt comfortable speaking Flemish in French-speaking areas. I remember how one day my father came to pick me up at school. The first thing I said was: "Please, dad, don't speak Flemish."

For some Walloons, this disdain might have changed in recent years due to the shifted political landscape in favour of the Flemings and its importance to finding a job. The Flemings are on the winning side be it economically as well as politically, and, due their uncompromising attitude and relentless ambition, inexorably gaining ground at all levels. The nationalist Flemish minister, Bart De Wever, who had caused so much upheaval in this country with his political party "the NVA" for an independent Flanders expressed his absolute disdain for any concern of the francophone people in these words to a francophone journalist: *"Ce qui est derrière moi, c'est mon cul!"* ("What's behind me is my arse!")

This took place after yet another fall out with his French-speaking counterparts in an attempt to form a government. There was time his *rondeurs* really looked so threatening and seemed to be filled with so much hate and rage, but he has slim down a lot recently making him less menacing even a bit softy. I hope that his love of French fries will bring those *rondeurs* back to their former glory again. This man was really a show on his own. It was fun to see him in action.

It is sometimes difficult to believe that La Wallonie, the francophone part of Belgium, was the economic power of this country until 1950. With their coal mines and steel and glass factories, cities like La Louvière, Charleroi, and Courcelles represented the livelihood of so many people in these regions and worked as a magnet for people, even from abroad. It was like a 'promised land.' It is estimated that more than 500.000 Flemings, fleeing poverty at home and leaving whole villages empty, migrated to these regions in order to find work. And with power came a certain haughtiness, which is one of the main characteristics that define Walloons. It was, I guess, a sad attempt to emulate their French counterparts: believing they represent the centre of the world.

It is true that Flemings were looked down upon and discriminated against, but they were not alone in that. This was the case for any foreigner who came to work there. Flemings had to wait until 1967 to see the Belgian constitution translated into Flemish despite it being the language of the majority of the people. This fact is still ignored by many people from outside Belgium. Some people even think that French is the only language in Belgium. Anyway, Walloon power is now but a distant memory. Nowadays, some francophone politicians who not that long ago would rather have killed themselves than speak Flemish in public are eager to show their skills in this once so hated language. Unfortunately, I do not think it matters anymore. It is payback time for the Walloon, and he damn well knows it!

I am racing ahead though; I was describing my life in the seventies in the Home Empain. I still have vivid memories of that place. I remember the time when all these little kids stood around a table with a little girl on it. She was awaiting her punishment, but she did not seem very concerned about was going to happen. Her confidence would soon subside though. The rest of us were debating how much of a spanking she deserved. I said 'two' and her brother Pascal opted for 'one'.

"After all, she is my sister" he said emotionally.

"What did you decided upon, kids?" our child minder, Carole, asked us when she came back, as if this was all a matter of fun. Frankly, I no longer recall what we decided, but this little girl who initially seemed to be so indifferent to what was about to happen to her started to shout and cry as Carole started to take her pants down.

Pascal was considered such an unruly kid at the Home; but when my parents invited him to our home one weekend, he was the loveliest kid anyone could imagine, as if utterly transformed. Sometimes I wonder what became of him. I still remember his mother, a prostitute and a fascinatingly beautiful woman, who had lost custody of her children.

This child minder, Carole, later became friends with my parents and was even invited all the way down to this backward town for our christening. It was quite an event the day the two little Negroes of the town got christened. Emotions ran high, and everyone seemed to be crying. A whole article was dedicated to it in a regional newspaper.

We stayed at this Home for one year only, and from there we went to a boarding school, called Don Bosco, in Jette (Brussels). Except for some of our caretakers and teachers, it was a school run mainly by nuns. It was quite common there to hear African kids being racially abused by the nuns. Perhaps what was most surprising was that anyone would have rather expected that from the caretakers or teachers instead of nuns. It was from their mouths I heard the first blatant racist insults. Despite this, I was happy there and felt secure. I spent practically all of my primary school years at Don Bosco. This place was a model for multiculturalism. It was something I had never seen before and have never seen since. The whole world seemed to be represented there, with many people from Congo and other African countries barely spoken of at the time. There were two brothers from Gabon: Landry and his younger brother Thierry. The latter apparently had an incontinence problem and still wet the bed, but the nuns found a solution for it: they made him wear a diaper. It was quite a sight seeing a kid about nine years old walking around the dormitory like that, his diaper bulging his pyjamas around his arse. Perhaps what was most striking was that he did not seem in any way embarrassed about it. There were also two brothers from Chad, Amir Adoudou and his younger brother Moussa. The latter I met a decade later in a most unusual circumstance: on our ways to the operation rooms, in a mainly Flemish-run hospital at the AZVUB in Jette. I was there for a knee operation. That day, the sight of two blacks teenagers going to the operation rooms simultaneously caused quite a sensation and was openly commented upon by just about everyone that saw us arriving.

"God what's happening here!" said one nurse, laughing aloud. I guess this must not have been such a daily occurrence. This childish excitement only put me under even more stress.

"Black people, what a disgusting race!" shouted Sister Jean-Marie one day at Don Bosco. I cannot remember what led her to say this, just as I have never come to comprehend why this sad creature had a man's name. I guess this must have been an integral part of her absurd existence. I think now that she was just been transferring her frustrations to black kids instead of their parents. There had been continued problems with African parents not providing the inscription money for their kids and, thus, leaving them to their own fate. It was not rare for the boarding school to take up the entire responsibility for some kids. Those kids even stayed there during the weekends, like unclaimed luggage.

I will never forget how one early evening Sister Jean-Marie came to a white kid's bed to put a suppository up him while we were still busy preparing ourselves to go to the shower room. We slept in one of those big dormitories without the slightest bit of privacy. She just put his blankets to one side, took his pyjamas down, and pulled up his butt cheeks in front of everyone; just like that, as if he was not supposed to feel in any way embarrassed about it. Perhaps what was most shocking was the banality of it all, as if she was rather dealing with an animal, a non-entity that was not bother with dignity. It did not go that smoothly though, and it took her a few attempts to finally get it in. Her glasses threatened to fall off every time she bent over to look for his arsehole as he laid on his side, waiting. He blushed and felt ashamed, as one could imagine, but I do not think this worried her one bit. If anything, she seemed to enjoy it. It was all a question of authority. Taking him somewhere more private would have taken all the fun out of it. Normally, they would have been far more people around to watch this disgusting spectacle but it happened on a Sunday and most people returned on Monday morning. I wonder whether these thoughts had not crossed her mind and, if by any chance, had not frustrated her.

The person we were most afraid was our principal, an Italian Sister named Stella. She had quite a temper. God, did she like to use her hands! Especially when the victim was not one of her favourites. I can testify to that. During my first year at the school, she took me and another black kid out of the queue because she had seen us talking. Then, without any warning, she started to beat us with her fists on our heads, which we tried to protect as best we could with our hands. She went ballistic, calling us *"les boudins noirs!"* (the Black puddings) while she kept beating us. Looking back at it, I am sure now she meant this rather as a sort of "initiation rite"; I had only been there for a few weeks. I will also never forget how one evening she held up high for everyone to see a Congolese kid's pyjamas that was full with skid marks, explaining to us in minute detail the benefits of knowing how to clean our arses.

"Otherwise," she added still holding up high the kid pyjamas so that everyone could have a good look at it, "you end up with such results."

The kid to whom the pyjamas belonged just did not know where to hide himself. It was if he wanted to disappear from the face of the earth. I know a few things about humiliations; I do not believe that anyone who has undergone such a public humiliation is likely to forget it for the rest of his life. Recently, I saw this evil creature in some old pictures of the school on Facebook. One former student on Facebook described his feelings this way: "Seeing that nun again brought back my worst nightmares." I shared the same feelings.

I can only thank God - in a manner of speaking of course, for I do not believe in Him - that we did not have any more men or priests around, particularly when I think of all the sexual abuse that was rampant in many such places. The only man was our sports teacher. During the last two years, things went from bad to worse. On one occasion, a Congolese guy named John was doing an exercise at the blackboard; as he got irritated at the way the teacher corrected him, he just turned around and slapped her in the face in front of everyone. The whole incident looked surreal to me, yet somehow he did not even get expelled for it. Despite his tender age, he had quite a high opinion of himself and was one of those Congolese kids who constantly bragged about everything their dad possessed. Africans, especially the Congolese, were the only ones to do that. The one thing that was maybe even more surreal was the fact that I finished first of my class my last year at the school.

It is difficult to explain what coming home every weekend to an all-white environment meant to me; the contrast could not have been more extreme. A lot of our social activities revolved around 'The Union' brass band that my parents were part of, the local football team, my music courses, and going to church. Actually, I stopped going to this stupid church by running ahead of my parents and going out through the back door.

"OK," said my mother wagging her finger at me, "You don't need to go to church any more, but I am warning you, Jesus is going to punish you." Sometimes Bruno and I, both in the uniform of the brass band, had to lead the way when the band was marching around the streets. This must have been a weird sight in those days. At the time, I still had not experienced the tension that comes from feeling like the odd one out and what that was supposed to mean. I was such a cute adorable little boy judging by the way people, especially women, enjoyed stroking my hair - as if I was some kind of dog. When I look back at it, one wonders who would not have liked to play with me.

During the first years at boarding school, I prayed to make the days go by faster so I could be home with my parents. Did I ever love this warm family nest and the sense of protection it offered me. We would sometimes invite some of the Congolese kids that stayed at school during the weekends to spend the weekend with us. This enthusiasm for coming home would die away during my last two years at school. I remember feeling a bit guilty about it for I worshipped my parents. These feelings had nothing to do with them: what was there to do at home anyway? I did not play with toy guns anymore, and the kids from school talked about how they roamed the streets during the weekends and did other more exciting things.

Once, Bruno and I tried to be part of a Flemish youth movement in this backward town called 'De Chiro,' but it turned out to be a complete farce as we got bullied away from it. The 'holiday camp' I went on was a nightmare from day one. The only thing on my mind had been getting back home again as soon as possible. I did not like playing football much either because of the uproar it provoked everywhere I showed up, as if I was some kind of freak. This happened more often when we did not play at home. Actually, the only team I liked to play against was a team from Peisegem because it had a black guy called Patrick. He also happened to be adopted. I also loved it when we had to play against a francophone team like Racing Jette from Brussels. These were rare occurrences though. I will never forget how two little girls around my age who were part of a visiting team once reacted when they saw us. "Buuurk! Two Negroes!" they shouted.

What was most hurtful was that their disgust seemed so honest and heartfelt. I quit playing football when I was about fourteen years old and decided to have a go at tennis instead, which I played during winter and summer. The only people I met from time to time in this town were outcasts; kids who seemed to be ignored by everyone else. Bruno was by far my only friend. I also enjoyed activities with my parents, especially during the summer when we went to the coast.

After my time at the boarding school, I went to College St. Pierre in Jette and came home every day. I met a friend there who also came from Don Bosco. Attending St. Pierre was quite an intimidating experience. The whole place had something cold about it. It was not at all multicultural and people were quite snobbish. On our first day, one teacher asked us to write the precise job of our parents on a piece of paper and hand it over to him. But first we had to say it aloud. I did not want to say that my father was a plumber, although he was already retired by then. He just kept working because he liked to stay active and also because had two more mouths to feed. Whenever I mentioned plumber it always conjured up images of someone trying to unclog a toilet with his hands deep in shit to his elbows. So I said that my father had two shops selling sanitary equipment, which he did when he was younger. One guy made everyone laugh when he said that his father was a window cleaner.

At the time, there were already constant scuffles, even fights, between Fleming and Walloon students. Whenever I came through the Flemish entrance to get to the playground, I knew beforehand that I would be called all kind of names by Flemish students. I stayed there two years, and from then on I started to drift from school to school as is often the case with dropouts. For a while, I did everything I could to try to stay in contact with some of the boys from boarding school. I missed them terribly. It felt like a security wall had been taken away from me. I felt lonely in this all-white world. For a while, we would meet each other once a year during the 'fancy fair;' an event with lots of activities organised by the school. For me, this was the biggest event of the year, but it died out after the first three years. I also went once on a weekend to the Ardennes with some of my former schoolmates from boarding school . Our leader had to change his planning completely after 'a little discussion' with my mother. I saw how from a distance she intimidated him. I guess she told him that I was neither allowed to go out nor drink any alcohol. I will never forget the way she wagged her finger at him, as if warning him, and how he just nodded his head; the poor guy. I had heard of these trips on how fun they were but, because of me, he had had to change a few things. The truth is that he was quite frustrated about it and, at one point, lashed his frustrations out on me during the weekend as if it was entirely my fault. Barely concealing his frustrations, he said to me: "Because of your mother, *j'ai dû tout changer!*" ("I had to change everything!")

My first year at the college St. Pierre was uneventful compared to the second, and even more on a personal level. There is no need to blame it on puberty because things were a bit more complicated than that to say the least.

During my second year, monsieur Dewallef, my maths teacher was the one who, on top of all other problems linked to the trials of

11

adolescence and being black, brought my fragile self-esteem to its lowest ebb. He always picked on me by saying things like: "Monsieur Lukemba, do not stay too long near the board it might make you turn white because of the chalk," "Monsieur Lukemba, watch out with your tippex (a brand of corrective fluid) it might leave some marks on you," or Monsieur Lukemba this, Monsieur Lukemba that. Perhaps it was never really racist, but just enough to make me look like a fool or feel inferior. He was not the only teacher to have such a strong sense of humour. I had to put up with some smart remarks from the others teachers as well. These were the eighties, but he just did not know when to stop. His highlight came during a photo session of our class. The pictures were taken in the refectory, which was full of students from other classrooms. At one point it was my turn to sit on the chair. Suddenly, he intervened excitedly to ask the photographer - loud enough for everyone to hear - to put more light on my face so that I would at least be visible on the picture. Even though I managed to keep my composure, it is easy to guess what went through my mind when the photographer instructed me to say 'cheese'!

I broke down in tears afterwards when I went to complain about it in the Principal's office. He was a priest. In retrospect, this must have been a desperately stupid thing to do, knowing what titillates these people. I might even have disturbed him about it whilst he went down memory lane. The fact is, I do not believe he ever talked this through with my maths teacher, and my parents did not want to make a fuss about it. My mum told me that my maths teacher was taken aback when, during a parents' teachers' conference, she told him about all the bullying he subjected me to. He pretended that he did not know what she was talking about. No doubt this must have given him carte blanche to take up his old habits.

While we were alone awaiting the arrival of the baldhead, monsieur Dewallef, I had a fight with a classmate. It changed people's perception of me completely. Not that I was bullied by my classmates or anything like that; the real bullies were the teachers, but it just surprised a lot of people. And probably even more so that it was for a stupid thing, really, and with a friend at that; one of the few guys I stayed in touch with for a while when I left this college. I cannot remember how it started, but I had punched his eye and it had swollen up. The baldhead noticed his eye and asked what had happened to it. Not wanting to be bother in trying to find out who started it first he sent us both to the Principal's office. On our way to his office, my friend began suddenly to cry, saying that it was all a misunderstanding and all that. It took my aback because I had always thought of him as a tough guy. It even embarrassed me seeing him cry like that. However, no matter what tough-guy image I was now basking in, it got constantly nullified by the baldhead's antics.

Yet one day, the baldhead amazed me in a positive way. Although it was not obligatory, I had been participating in an extra class on a Saturday, reviewing for the exam ahead. We had to solve a complicated algebra exercise and I happened to be the only one who made a successful attempt to resolve it.

"Oh," he said in front of the class, showing much understanding to all those who failed in their attempt to solved it, "only Monsieur Lukemba would have been able to do it anyway." This took me completely by surprise; I could not believe that this arsehole had been monitoring my progress in maths. I wonder what demons possessed him that pushed him to pick on me like that. The fact he was bald at quite a young age? He had this profound sadness about him of people who try to hide their baldness by combing their few remaining hairs from one side to the other. I remember how one day a student had said something funny about his baldness. Our maths teacher turned as read as a tomato and touched immediately his remaining hair as if to make sure they were still laying the way he had combed them.

That year, I started to discover music in a more passionate way. I loved this new wave music, and the guy I had fought with always gave me some cassette tapes. It was also a time in my life when people began to talk about the parties they planned to go to. Some of these parties were the talk of the day, and of course, I wanted to be part of them too. However, the only thing that was awaiting me was a

13

dead boring weekend in this Flemish town where I had no friends at all. I could not bear to hear people talk on a Monday about how some party had been, or even hear them talk about their weekend. I always envied my classmates for being part of civilisation. My mother would not have it any other way as she did not want me to go out. When later on, although this happened rarely, I was allowed from time to time by my parents to go out with friends from Brussels to a party and crash at a friend's place, the most depressing thing was always when I had to come back to this depressing town.

From that school, I went on to Cardinal Mercier in Schaerbeek (Brussels) where I had a go at woodwork. I hated it just as much as I hated that school. Actually, it is still the only school where I was scared to pass in front of a group of teachers for fear of being publicly humiliated. One of them, though not my teacher, once asked me laughing at the way I handled pieces of wood: "Where do you think you are, in the jungle?"

Another person who liked teasing me with funning comments was a priest; l'Abbé Wynant, my religion teacher. I hated this fascist pig! When we had to smile politely and laugh at one of his sad jokes, he would raise his finger as if warning me and say: "Don't you laugh you too at this joke, it might turn you white." He did this almost every time. While he was walking in the corridors, he had seen me laughing during another teacher's course by looking through the glass panel of the door of our classroom. "I saw you had a lot of fun," he said when he met me later with other students on the stairs. Then, he threatened to slap me in my face in front of everyone.

By far the most depressing thing was the way I had to go back and forth to this school. I had to get off the bus once it entered Laeken and from there take a tram to Schaerbeek. The area where I got off the bus was a Flemish area at the outskirts of Brussels, the periphery. In fact, it was already Brussels, but in no way would anybody get the feeling of actually being in Brussels. The worst part was the journey back. To take the bus back to this backward town, I would meet all these white Flemish students coming from their all-white schools and returning to their all-white Flemish towns. They

14

seemed to enjoy it to flash their 'terrified faces' once they noticed me arriving to the bus stop. This alone, setting aside all of the other problems, was hurtful and depressing. So, in order not to give them all these thrills for free, I took a tram nearby my school to anywhere in the centre of Brussels; then from there, take the bus that would bring me back to my town. I also found out that in the same area where I met all these 'terrified faces' that there was another bus stop but with not so many people around it, with a bus that went through my town. The timetable and the itinerary were obviously different, with fewer buses and a longer overall trip. Yet I would take this in my stride rather than be confronted again with these 'terrified faces' at the other bus stop. Another Congolese friend who I met at College St. Pierre also lived in the same kind of backward Flemish town (Grimbergen) as I did, but his was even closer to Brussels. He told me how he and his younger brother were humiliated every day on the bus. It got so out of hand one day that he decided to face his bullies and threatened to beat them up. It worked: they never bothered him again!

As one can imagine, daily strain like this from dawn to dusk was wearing me down and could only lead to a mental breakdown. Not to mention my crippling low self-esteem and the identity problem I was facing. The world outside was certainly not a nice place to live in. All of this started to strain relations at home. I tried to kill myself by swallowing a whole bunch of sleeping pills that I had received from a fellow student at school. I do not think he had the slightest idea of what my real intentions were, nor did I ever talk to him about what happened afterwards. When they woke me up, I started to cry out of frustration for still being alive. My mum, who must have felt helpless, asked for advice to our family doctor.

After this crisis, a psychiatrist - a Walloon - was recommended. Her name: Francine Dal. She was someone that through the common language would enable me to better express myself. She worked at the AZVUB hospital in Jette. Before that, we had gone to another shrink, a man, in the city of Mechelen in Flanders. I do not remember how we came to him, but I liked his sessions. Finally, here was someone who listened to me and was impartial. No wonder my mother said she did not like him much. She could not play her usual tricks on him; tricks she would play with verve on that woman. During one of these visits, while I sat in the waiting room ruffling through magazines, I came across a regional newspaper with a full page article about my father, August Hellemans, ex-captain of the 'Red Devils,' the national Belgian football team. He had been the first Red Devil from KV Mechelen to be selected for the national team and he captained the Red Devils during their first world championship in Montevideo in Uruguay. This was my father they were talking about. I am aware this is a coincidence that sounds too good to be true, yet it is! And I am sure that this young psychiatrist at the time could still confirm that, despite the fact that this had happened so many years ago. He could not but have noticed this local newspaper lying in his waiting the room with this great front-page picture of my father with his hat on. Neither can I imagine that he forgot about me, given the strangeness of my case.

In those days, I was about 14 years old, it was common to walk in Mechelen all day long without coming across a single black person. I once met a guy from Togo who came to live there in his teens, straight from his home country. He told me that even in 2000, there were only a few blacks and that they basically all knew each other. Nothing, he added, comparable to what it is now. People from a younger generation may have a hard time believing this. Yet they just need to ask older people around them. How could that be made up anyway? How can I explain to younger people all the excitement I once caused in this city when my parents dropped me off at a movie theatre to join the queue for the James Bond movie 'Never Say Never Again'?

The psychiatrist suggested to my parents that I stay at the hospital for some things she had in mind. After a few private sessions with her, she came to the conclusion that I was a bit strange, somehow different. I had told her that, when I was at boarding school at Don Bosco, I had prayed once to make the days go by faster and that to my surprise it had worked: it had indeed become

16

Friday. This must have been a fascinating way to assess someone's mental state! Looking back at it, I must have been a godsend to her, or for anyone else for that matter, to indeed have someone a bit different on which to apply all these imbecilic theories she learned at school. I do not think that she had much opportunity there to scrutinize the brain of a Negro. What did someone like that know about people from other ethnic backgrounds at the time? Everyone knows that most of these psychiatrists are completely mad - it is not even a cliché - with their depressing bullshit about stuff like psychoanalysis.

So it started with a one-week stay that was followed by a second week and then a third drugged-filled week on Haldol. I still do not know what good it was supposed to have done, since the only effect it had on me was keeping me dizzy for most of the time. This place was hell on earth! When after one week I was allowed to go home for a weekend, I begged my mother not to send me back there, but my attempts were futile. I had to go. It could have been that she had no say in it. They finally seemed to have found the solution: I needed Haldol! Like Harry-Potter magic, this was supposed to stop people from pointing their fingers at me, erase their disgust at the sight of me, stop them from hurling insults, and thus alleviate the strain I was constantly under. All thanks to Haldol! How on earth was this white woman going to understand what the fuck I was going through? How on earth was I going to explain to her that the simple fact of getting out of my home, that had somehow become a prison, made me fearful and put me under stress? No word was said about my isolation. There was no mention anywhere that my main problem could have been a predominantly geographical one, a problem of finding oneself totally isolated. What the fuck was I doing in this god-forsaken backward town where I knew no-one, outside civilisation and among one of the most backward species on earth! Most of my problems would not even have existed had this place been part of civilisation. I do not believe that she, a Walloon, did not know anything about the backwardness and ingrained racism of Flemish people. Just the name of this town, which I will never reveal, said it

17

all. Decades later, I saw this psychiatrist on television being interviewed on child protection. It sent shivers down my spine.

My school year at Cardinal Mercier turned out to be a complete farce. I failed in every subject. Despite this, I started to feel better. Things could only get better after everything I had gone through until then. It was holiday time, and I felt relief that I did not have to go this school anymore. I contacted some old friends from Brussels with whom I had lost touch. While staying at a friend's apartment I decided to get a fashionable haircut, like Grace Jones, and my ears pierced so I could wear an earring. I also received from my friend a military jacket, thus completing my new-wave look.

"This should do it," I thought to myself. I felt so real, like people do when they think they fit the profile regarding what is fashionable. That was the mind of a fifteen or sixteen year old speaking.

As per a previous arrangement, my mother was going to pick me up. When she saw me coming, she was visibly shocked.

"What happened to your hair, this earring, what's this jacket?" she asked when I entered the car. "What's all this about! I hope you are not going to wear this around town, are you? What are people going to say?" I got angry and stepped again out of the car, not minding my destination. She followed me in her car and kept honking at me while I stood there waiting for a tram. A Congolese man witnessed this and persuaded me to show some respect and to listen to her. So I went back inside the car, still obviously cross.

It was upon getting home that the real drama unfolded. First, there was an emergency call to be made to her friend for some advice. It had to be done quickly! Her relationship with her 'friend' was one in which this old witch would call my mum by her first name and my mum would call her 'miss.' This old witch was an incredibly sad, pathetic creature. She found everything about herself interesting and, thus, thought she was at the centre of the world. It was at her home that Bruno and I followed catechism courses. Another precaution my mother took was to warn the neighbourhood about my hair, claiming that I had been sick and had to have it cut that way. This old witch, my mother's friend, suggested calling my shrink to see

18

what she might have to say about it. Since I had left the hospital I had an appointment once a week with my shrink, but this was a matter too urgent to leave until the next appointment; so that same day, we went to my psychiatrist. Upon our arrival, my mum found an opportunity to play her trick, the one that had always worked until then: cry endlessly.

"Look at him! Look at his clothes, his hair!" she exclaimed to my shrink. I instinctively felt that my shrink was not going to take into account anything I may have to say in my defence, nor was she going to play down the whole thing by saying things like:

"Wait a minute, let me get this straight. So you brought your son here because of his haircut and dress sense, right?"

This would have ridiculed my mother and tarnished her halo of sanctity. When it was my turn to speak and I explained that I was just trying to comply with a certain style of music that I was very passionate about, my shrink was visibly shocked. I immediately felt that I had said too much. She looked at me, and after a while, came to the conclusion that I was talking so 'strangely' again. So, out of regard for what people might say and because of my "strange talk," I got locked up for three weeks during summer holidays with their 'miracle cure' at hand. After I had to give away what my shrink called 'this dirty jacket,' I went into my room and broke down in tears.

Later, at the suggestion of my shrink, I was sent to a sports camp in Herbeumont, in the Ardennes. I have often wondered how my mother - I will still call her that - justified my three week absence during summer holidays to people who asked after me. No one ever really talked to me about that, so I wonder whether she hid this or only told her hard core fans about it, I mean the ones that were convinced of her sanctity. Anyway, this would come back to haunt her implacably in due time.

Chapter 2

Mixing with "normal people"

Things at home changed in a way that could not have been more extreme: I started to mingle with people from here, from that town. Not with outcasts anymore, but with 'normal people.' They were the people I had once fantasized about having as friends one day when I observed them passing in front of the window of my home. It was so exciting! I had always imagined what exciting lives they must be leading, being amongst friends and all that. I had envied these boys because of all the things they were allowed to do. Well, they certainly did not stir things up the way I did because of the effect of the colour of my skin wherever I showed up in town.

A friend of Bruno's, a Congolese lad, came over for one week to crash at our place. One day we went with him to a park where in no time, we were the centre of attention. We got into a conversation with other youths, some of whom I already knew by sight when I had to play football against their team. The next day we returned to the same place and started to befriend and go out with some of them. The same way it goes as in any other place in the world. As was to be expected, this time my mother did not mind when I went to parties because she knew most of the boy's parents, and the very fact that they were from our town reassured her. I still remember how embarrassed I was when one young lad asked my mother who we used to hang out with.

"No-one!" said my mother. "They knew no-one," she reiterated. She was right! This time I really enjoyed and exploited my status as 'exotic,' the odd one out. Well, most of the time anyway.

During that same period, I also had a girlfriend, and on top of that, I went to a school I really enjoyed: L'école St.Ursule in Laeken. It was all too extreme for word; these extremes would always be at the core of my life. It always went from one extreme to another. Whether or not I contributed to it does not really matter. During my first year at this school, I remember how proud my parents were of my results, and how my father held me in his arms after a meeting with the teachers. I was allowed, as a present, to go with friends on a holiday to Spain, which was quite an experience. I do not think that the Spaniards would like to hear it but, back then, Spain was basically a third world country. However, it would be a bit over the top to compare it to any African state. With little money, a tourist from Belgium could live there like God in France, but I do not think the Spaniards wanted this to be the case for me. Judging by the look on their faces, they could not understand what was happening to them. Truth be told, it was not just the Spaniards, but just about everyone. Even the guys I was with started to feel a bit annoyed by it. I guess people expected me to sell things rather than be on holiday! I was 17 years old at that time, but I probably looked far younger. We slept in a tent on a camp-site, and we went to the most posh restaurants and trendy bars we could find at night.

I spent two years at St. Ursule before I got expelled. In my later years, I dated a girl who was in the same class with me at the time. I could not believe it when she revealed to me that, after having leaving school, she dated our former French language teacher, who was married and had a child. He is now the mayor of a certain town in Brussels. She always seemed to have had a weakness for more 'mature' men. Once, she even dated - or, as she told me, 'stayed in contact with' - a guy 25 years older than her. Apparently, things are never quite as they seem. I should be the first to know.

It was during my second year at St. Ursule that my relationship with my mother, through a mix of things in which I am certainly not entirely blameless, deteriorated to a point of no return. My exoticness also seemed to have worn off a bit among the youth I had befriended in this town.

Marc was friend I came to learn in my teens in this Flemish town. Life had not always been easy for him too. His sister had married an Arab, which in these regions is, to put it mildly, not really recommended. This Arab had come to Belgium in his teens. After their marriage, he lived with her on the same street as I did. Thanks to his father-in-law, a cop, he found work. In the summer, he liked to show off driving around on his Harley. This Arab must have laughed at his luck. I am sure that his family back home in his native Algeria spoke of him as a hero. Marc and his sister were actually from Meise, but they spent most of their lives in this town where they were practically raised by their grandparents. For my mother, the way Marc's parents seemed to wash their hands of him and then spoil him out of guilt, had always been a never ending exciting topic of conversation. During the World Cup in Mexico, Marc and I watched the Belgians play against Argentina in a local pub. Later that night, he came to crash at my place. While looking around my room, all of sudden he said:

"In fact, you haven't got anything you can really call your own, do you?"

He must have been looking at the pictures on the walls. They were pictures of dogs, wild animals, or things of a similar nature my mother used to hang up whenever she came across one she fancied. It later became a big issue when I tried to take them off or even simply move some stuff from one place to another. Like the day I had moved old board games from my room into the attic. My mother was so shocked that I had not consulted her about it first that she brought them back from the attic and put them back on the shelves in my room.

I was struck by his observation because before that I had never paid much attention to all these things. For sure, there must have been a few occasions in the past that might have made me aware of it, but until then, it had not really bothered me. On top of that I had friends now, led a normal life like any teenager, and was allowed to go on holiday to Spain. So why bother about all these pictures and shit? Yet, for him to have made such an observation at such a young age - he was only sixteen at the time, I was a year older - strikes me to this day. He was damn right!

Around that same period, his sister told me how every time she dreaded to go back home in Meise. She always felt like a thief because of the way her mother and stepfather would stare at her, watching her every move whenever she had to take something from the cupboard. Ironically, even I was shocked by what she told me, as if I had never experienced anything similar. It is only when I stopped playing along and grew tired of keeping up appearances that I came to perfectly understand what she meant. Although it must have been nothing in comparison to what she ever experienced. In my case, it triggered the complete breakdown of family life. What tired me most was having to put this infantile smile on my face for no reason at all, this happy clown face, having constantly to show people how grateful I was to have them as parents.

My mother loved this smile, as most white people do. It was non-threatening and had a kind of innocence about it, but by far the most important thing was that she could pass it off as a sign of sexual immaturity. Well, in her overheated mind anyway. Like most people whose sole obsession is sex, despite their veneer of respectability, this was the image of me she liked best and wanted me to convey to the people of this town: that of a totally sexless human being. It was a bit like in the antebellum South where Negroes were still called 'boy' at the age of forty, or 'uncle,' in a desperate attempt to make them forget about their reproductive organs and to deny them any manhood. Yet I soon had to deal with her pent-up sexual fantasies and debilitating sexual problems.

I do not know much about the sex lives of mature women and, to be honest, I am quite happy about that. Little do I care that some mature women may have a fascinating sexual life and still be interested in sex, contrary to what people generally think. The subject does not fascinate me much, no matter how hard the media in its unrelenting quest for gender-equality, tries to portray mature women as sexy. I am not getting any younger myself, and there will probably come a time when I will have to indulge in mature sex too. For now, I just hope I can put this predicament on hold. For some reason I like freshness. The fact is, my mum was still relatively young and must have had her own needs. It seemed to intrigue her that anyone would wash themselves entirely naked in front of a wash bowl. In her mind, cleanliness is something that could be seen instantly, like a clean house, clean clothes. This was in perfect keeping with her hypocrisy. Why bother about more intimate things? My mum must also have been titillated at the thought of her favourite pet, who had grown up now, standing there naked. So she would stand close to the door every morning - I could see her head through the glass panel of the door - and amuse herself by brutally opening the door without any warning to ask me not to forget to take out the plug from the boiler or any other stupid excuse. Whenever I complained, she would laugh at me and try to demean me by saying:

"What's the problem? I washed your arse so many times when you were little."

This whore seems to have lost every ounce of self-respect. I began to say things a person does not normally say to a mother. "Why don't you buy yourself a dildo?" I asked her once.

So I started to wear a towel around my waist every morning, except when I took a bath because then I could close the door from inside. Even when I went to pee, I would make sure I closed the door of the bathroom firmly because I could not lock it from inside. She would then sometimes fake that she was going to open it. Perhaps the most incredible thing was that after yet another shouting match with her, without any sense of shame, she would stand in the frame of the door playing 'the concerned mother' to wave me goodbye on my way to school when the bus came by. Who would ever believe that of such an upright citizen who was so highly regarded by everyone in this town? She knew that she could get away with these sorts of things, thanks to her standing in the community. When I asked her why she needed to stay at the front door to wave me goodbye, she replied that she was waving at an acquaintance. It was only after much insisting that she quit playing this sad comedy. It made me look like a fool, a mummy's boy.

Family life, if you could still call it that, had become a hopeless farce. Whenever she came home from shopping and I happened to be around, she would try to find a way to hide her wallet. One of her tricks would be to walk around the table and, from the moment she thought I was not looking, put her wallet on the chair and then push it back under the table. Another was to send me to her sleeping room to close the window so that she would have enough time to hide her wallet. I once found out, while I was playing piano, that she even put it behind the piano desk. I only noticed it when she came directly to retrieve it in a manner she thought was very subtle. Whenever she thought she had lost something, she would moan and moan endlessly, complaining that this happened time and again around here. If she thought I could not hear her, she would say it even more loudly until the whole thing died down. Only then did I know that she had found it, as usual. There had never been any reason for all this mistrust. But, in fact, I had always been considered a thief. It started from an early age when I was still in boarding school and was allowed to come home on Wednesday afternoons. One day, upon coming home from football training, Bruno and I had to sit around the table because she claimed that her jewellery had been stolen.

"Someone has stolen my jewellery," she said, "and obviously it can only be one of you."

Bruno and I looked at each other with utter disbelief. On my part, I was too stunned to say anything. After sometime, Bruno mustered the courage to say something, but she immediately hushed him back to silence with a hand gesture. I never heard her mention it again, so she must have found it, as always. To be fair, I do not think it ever crossed her mind that this could be hurtful or undermine any normal relationship. On the contrary, the next minute, she expected me to play 'happy family' again - or what was rather left of it - as if nothing ever happened. This is really too sad for words! Even the fact that I would get out of bed early in the morning during the weekends would raise her suspicions and make her wake up too.

There came a time when I stopped taking offence at all this. I had become mute and barely spoke, which drove her mad, insane even. One day, she deliberately pushed her vacuum cleaner against my toes in order to make me say something; it really hurt me, yet I did not say anything. Another time, she came threateningly close to me with the fryer. I could hear the oil still boiling and thought she may deliberately let it fall on my feet. She would also try to get a reaction

26

from me by giving excessive amounts of food to our dog knowing this would make him sick and throw up, because in her demented mind I was supposed to pay more attention to the dog than my father. That is how low this crazy woman had sunk. I came to know she had cancer when she came into my room one evening, attempting to put the blame on me. I did not know what to think at first because it was possible she was making it up. If not, I was certainly hoping the diagnosis was correct. Did that not mean she was going to die, and that there would be an end to all this madness? I still wonder what her friend must have thought when she came back with her from the hospital one day, all excited about the fact that the cancer was in remission and thinking I was going to share her enthusiasm. I could not care less. If anything, for me, this was bad news, and she must have read it on my face.

As a student, I worked during the summer on Sundays at the marketplace near the South Station in Brussels, selling shoes with an acquaintance of my parents. Sometimes, I brought home Arab pancakes. When I sat at the table and my father saw me eat, he would want to eat too, even if he had just finished eating. He had become bulimic and did not stop eating. The poor man was suffering from Alzheimer's, and his health had gone from bad to worse. There was quite a big age difference between my mother and him. Seeing him constantly eating like that was an awful sight. I tried to stop him by taking the sugar out of his hands, but neither did I want to be too brutal about it. I was scared of what this woman might think. After all, in her sick mind, she thought I was mistreating him behind her back. I could not believe it when one day she noticed that he had a scratch on his forehead and loudly said so I could hear:

"Oh God, who did that to you?"

So, not really knowing what to do, I just sat there. This woman had been watching all then and came rushing from the kitchen with an accusing glance for letting that happen. She turned to me and said:

"You damn well know he isn't allowed to eat that much!"

She then pretended to cry. Her whole intention was to place a bombshell - "Mistreatment of a Vulnerable Old Person" - at my feet and then tell her friends about it. Yet she knew that I missed my father as I had once told her. I guess she must have felt a bit ashamed of her behaviour because that evening, while I sat in my room as usual, she came to say that there was a good movie on the telly. I could not wait to join her.

She had become so desperate about the whole situation that when my social worker came around, among the usual complaints that included me not doing well at school - which was true - and a total lack of communication, she also criticized my vegetarian food which she found too expensive. This seemed quite ironic. Her biggest fears, which amounted to obsessions, had always been drugs and alcohol. Although such imbeciles always need to be worked up about something, I did none of that. I turned veggie when I was seventeen years old till my thirty. If anything, it helped to discipline me. I am not saying that I never smoke a joint or drink beer, but it is rare which seemed to surprises - even deceived - a lot of people, whites as well as blacks. As if I no longer looked that cool with my dreadlocks, but rather fake.

During all these troubled years because of all this tension, Bruno and I did not speak to each other. My stubbornness in not wanting to change anything to that - well, at least on my part anyway - was to deny my mother any semblance of family life that would vindicate her. Bruno had become as foreign to me as anyone who might read this. When Bruno came home during the weekend from university, my mum would sometimes try to find an occasion to put up a good scene, knowing that I was not going to say anything anyway.

One day, she said to Bruno with a face of endless suffering, "If you only knew half of what happens when you aren't here."

Well, I knew what it was: the most destructive, suffocating, toxic place on earth. When I came home, I would prepare my vegetarian food and then go directly to my room in order to avoid any physical contact. Only rarely would I go to watch a movie in the living room where my father was lying. The poor man had fallen off the stairs and we had to place a bed there. He went to sleep every day at around 8 pm. While sitting on his bed, she sometimes tried to seek contact and get me to talk. Once, among other things, she asked why I did not pay any attention to my father.

"He didn't do anything bad to you!" she once said.

It might appear that way that I did not pay any attention to my father, but this was not the case. Foremost, I did not want this to be an excuse to unite us or to be seized upon by her because of the situation we were in. Anyway, too much had happened. Besides, how was I supposed to show my father any affection and at the same time mistreat him?

Maybe there was also another reason, which I too vividly remember. Once when I was a boy, I went to buy a toy for Bruno with my mum. I cannot remember what the occasion was, but it was not for his birthday.

"Look here," she said "He's going to buy a little present for his brother. Isn't that beautiful?" she asked the shopkeeper. Then, in a pathetic scene of sentimentality, she tried to cry. The only reaction she got from the woman shopkeeper was a look as if to say:

"What's gotten into this woman?" I was totally embarrassed.

I had definitely quit school by now, without any qualifications, and so I started to look for work. I do not think this worried my mother the slightest. School had become a complete farce long ago. I just went to school to spend the day. My first attempts to find work were not successful but finally, thanks to an acquaintance of my mother, I found work as a handyman on a six months contract at a care home which was part of the OCMW (Public Centre for Social Action) in my town. It eased tensions between us a bit, and taking up her role of 'the concerned mother' again, she would sometimes pass by my workplace to bring me some fruit or other things. I turned a blind an eye to that. This woman really knew how to cast herself! Nine years later, during my second stint at this care home, people still talked about it.

"Your mum was such a lovely person!" they said. However, tensions flared up again once my contract was over. With this on-going uncertainty regarding my future, and Bruno still at the

29

university, this was somewhat to be expected. But more than anything else, it was the sexual tension deriving from the promiscuity at home that had become unbearable and suffocating. I could barely look at her without her making feel threatened as if I had to feel guilty somehow for any of her sexual fantasies about me; or did she maybe feel guilty about some of the things that could so easily have been avoided? That sounds rather like wishful thinking on my part. I constantly had to be careful with the way I handled myself. When I watched the telly, lying on the couch with my hand on my crotch, she would notice this and try to find out whether I had a hard on. Looking back at it, this woman must have felt permanently threatened. I sometimes wonder how many times the thought of being raped must have crossed her mind with two black males around and a father who was going completely gaga due to his Alzheimer's. There must have been moments when she realised that, in the end, we were complete strangers to her. It is only long afterwards that I realised how strange this situation must have been for her.

Her health was not getting any better either. It had gone from bad to worse as she went in and out at a hospital in Bonheiden. I had visited her twice, but I still did not have a clue that time was running out for her until the day a niece called me to say that she was probably going to die and asked me if I could come over. I could not care less and had been quite brutal on the phone. It did make me feel guilty when I met this woman at the funeral. In the end, I went to see my mum along with Bruno and a cousin. She had been given a slight shot of morphine and was half unconscious when we arrived there. I was shocked when she seemed to regain consciousness all of a sudden and asked for me to open the window.

"Don't you worry about that, just die" I thought to myself, even though I did as she told me. I stayed there alone in the room with her after Bruno had left. My cousin, a son of my father's sister, was going to pick me up later that night. It was quite spooky seeing life drain away from her and notice her skin turn paler and paler. I had never witnessed someone dying before. She was still breathing when my cousin came back to pick me up. I could see by the way he looked at me that he had expected me to be in a more emotional state, as if I had been crying or something. What he was faced with instead must have been a picture of sheer indifference. My mum finally died in the early morning. Amen.

Chapter 3

"Ne Me Quitte Pas" (song from Jacques Brel)

It was a beautiful day to bury my mother. I cannot describe how elated I felt, this sense of relief walking behind her hearse. I laughed and could barely believe my luck. I thought:

"This whore is finally dead! God Save the Queen! I would have buried her with my own hands if I had to, just to make sure she lay in there.

I hated this woman! The truth is that if I could have killed her and gotten away with it, by lacing her drink or food, I would probably have done so. I certainly would not have regretted it for one minute in my life. Her death is by far one of the most ecstatic moments I have known in my life and one of the most intense orgasms I have ever experienced. I am less afraid of dying than of seeing that woman again. On our way back from the cemetery, I was approached by an old toothless woman.

"I know that this may not be the right time to ask such a thing, but do you know already anything about the house?" she asked. It took me aback because it shocked me that these were the kinds of thoughts that were on her mind in such moments. "No," I replied. Until then, I had never given much thought to that. She was from Impde, a nearby village, and was family of my mum. The only reason I remembered her was because of her teeth, or rather, the lack of it. As a boy, I had accompanied my mother when she went to visit her. During all the time I was there, I had been watching her mouth as if mesmerized. I could not understand why she did not bother to put in false teeth. Decades later, she still seemed to have done nothing about having some teeth in her mouth.

I know how fortunate and indebted I am to my adoptive parents for having taken Bruno and I under their wing. They went out of their way to give us a decent life. My father's money days had been well and truly over when he took all the necessary steps to be granted custody over us. He had once owned six houses. Life without them would have been even more bleak and desperate. But that did not give my mother special rights to think that I was like beholden to her and therefore was allowed to do everything with me what she had in mind. I am still wrapped in guilt about some of the things I said, like: "You are not my mother."

It was imbecilic, sad, and desperately low, even though I said this more for its dramatic effect. I still regard them as my only true parents; I never gave a shit about my biological parents. I am also aware of how tough and overwhelming things must have been for them, especially for my mum, in such a narrow-minded community. I'm afraid that for some things they were ill-prepared. But as much as anyone else, she enjoyed all this gossip, rumours, et cetera, and maybe was she the greatest hypocrite of them all. It is sometimes difficult to believe that she wanted me to show an interest for all this gossip, too. The meanness, hypocrisy of people in these Flemish towns, especially the falseness of women and the way they revel in each other's misery, defies the imagination. My mum's main intellectual activity was peering through the window and whenever she thought people might see her, she would back down a bit. She could spend hours commenting on everything she saw happening on the street. About 'the one who had just left his wife,' or 'the other who was a drunk.'

I wonder how haunting and confusing it must have been for her, from the moment I could be considered a grown up man and, therefore, a sexual being. Me, her favourite pet! In order to allay her fears, she did as much as she could to infantilise me. High on her agenda was to pass me off as someone hopeless and immature in order to justify her overbearingness. At the same time, she also tried to convey to her friends a certain (sexual) distance that had always supposedly been between us. From early on it seems, she had been trying to neutralise me sexually by suggesting I become a good a priest when I grew up. The reason also why it did not bother her - she actually even encouraged me to - to see me work in her cousin's

34

gay pub was another attempt from her to convey this sexual distance. Maybe did she hope that way that by working in this pub someone would convert me into a sissy and thus have a 'girlfriend' to talk to making me even less threatening to her.

Some women actually enjoy the company of gay men more than that of their own kind. By the way, I never went to work in this gay pub or any gay pub for that matter. By contrast, when Bruno worked as a teenager at a gas station in Brussels, and my mum happened to see this homosexual she had heard about, she came rushing out of the car all panic. Yet this homosexual was like any other customer that came there and often enjoyed having a chat with Bruno without therefore harassing him. Although I did not realise it at the time, I am absolutely convinced that my mother saw me as some kind of companion with whom to share her old days with. Actually, this might even have been an idea she had been nurturing since I was a little kid. As a child, I once talked to her about getting married and other related topics of that nature.

"Why would you get married?" She replied, "You have already got me as a wife."

Looking back at it, it was certainly not that innocent, and me being a sissy of some sort would have made it more respectable to the outside world. To be frank, I do not think it would have been that morally wrong to see me as a companion or husband either whether or not I would have turned into a 'sissy'. If Woody Allen could marry his adopted daughter, what would have been so wrong in her doing the same? One day, I was preparing my luggage to stay over at a friend's house for a weekend. Not knowing what I had in mind, she started to cry as if I was leaving her for ever. "Where are you going?" she kept asking.

The thought of growing old alone must have driven her mad. I am still wondering how she was trying to work that out after all we had been through. She once told a couple that came to visit me that I was not there, even though they had seen me passing by. This couple, Els and Werner, were close Flemish friends with whom I used to go to festivals and reggae concerts. I knew nothing about it at the time;

they only told me after she had died. It made them laugh, adding: "She was probably scared of losing you."

They were not a couple in the way we think. She was about twenty-two years old and he was a bit older. Werner was rather like her slave really, which must have had a castrating effect on him. Els, quite the dominant type, did not care about him as much as he wanted her to, and she used to humiliate him in public at the slightest occasion. But this sad clown was so crazy about her that he did not mind. Or maybe did he just enjoyed to be dominated as it is the case for so many white men. He later turned 100% gay. I found this quite confusing at the time. "How could he be so crazy about a woman and at the same time be a closeted homosexual," I thought. Yet there were rumours. A friend, who also used to join us at concerts and reggae parties, always got irritated by his effeminate manners. What most irritated him was the way he would pass his hand through his hair like girls do and therefore called him 'mevrouw Werner' (mevrouw means 'miss'). Little did I know at the time that it was exactly what he would turn out to be: a miss. He managed to get rid of his homosexuality, so to speak, by becoming a transsexual. Clever boy! He is still the only person I have known quite well to have undergone such an operation.

People like to romanticize overprotective, overbearing mothers, while all too easily overlooking how ruthless and selfish they can be. The truth is that these kind of moms don't acknowledge the aspirations and needs of their kids as long as they do not suit their own. I will never forget how one day that demented woman came barging into my room after a female friend had put a letter into our letterbox to postpone a rendezvous. She was not even my girlfriend but just a friend. I never had the chance to read that letter because my mother refused to give it to me, although I could easily guess what the content was.

"She looked like a scarecrow!" she said, still fuming.

Everything was always perceived as a threat to my mum. Having a bit of intimacy, whether alone or with friends, was always a struggle for me. Whenever I was on the phone she would try to eavesdrop. If I sat with friends in the living room, she would come by every five minutes to look at what we were doing, which would then irritate me and make me go to my room. Still, the next minute, she would come by there, too, under the pretence of asking us not smoke. It was only afterwards that I wondered whether she thought we might be doing anything more than just talking, especially when I was alone with a friend. When a girlfriend she knew quite well from town came to our home for a bit of cosiness and to watch Dynasty with me, she would come by every five minutes to ask us whether we needed some more coffee or biscuits. I thought that my girlfriend would see through her comedy; but no, she found my mum such a lovely person. One night I came back with a girl I met during a concert of the reggae group Yellowman in Holland. In the morning when they met each other, despite my mother's surprise, she stay friendly and even invited my girlfriend to eat something. But before I went back to Brussels with my girlfriend, she opened the door to look all around her to see if the coast was clear making sure that no one saw me in the company of a girl. Afterwards, she asked me to stay far away with 'all this.' She did not want me to convey an image of sexuality and, as such, with needs of my own. This was something I had to play out far from view of the people of this town. In this town, I had to pass myself off as a cuddly eunuch to prevent any sexual connotations in relation to her, which were bound to happen in such a small-town anyway. For Bruno, this was rather ok because he was the studious one and was successful at school. Also, his relation with my mother was totally different because she never set her sights on him the way she did with me. I was her favourite pet and future companion.

Poor woman, I am so glad she died. If I had not shouted or bit at her, I would probably still be sitting on her lap. She never really came to terms with the fact that I grew up. Like so many white people who adopted a little monkey, she expected me to stay like Webster; the little black boy in the American TV series who was adopted by white middle-class parents, or like Arnold Jackson in Different Strokes - something cute anyway. Come to think of it, I am quite glad that her

English was not that good. Who knows if on top of other things like wanting me to behave childishly in order not to feel threatened and be a cuddly eunuch, she may have asked me to say Arnold's catchphrase (*"whatchoo talkin 'bout, Jesus?"*) too while I would be sitting on her lap and make these big eyes. A word of advice to the Madonna's and mother Theresa's of this world planning to adopt a little black monkey of the opposite sex: beware, it does grow and grow, and you can do nothing to stop it.

The one thing that still haunts me to this day is a picture of her with my father on his eightieth birthday. She was smiling, but it was a forced smile. I could tell, especially because of those eyes. God, those eyes! They were ones of desperation, a sense of total abandonment and disillusionment with everything. She liked to say that I was taking advantage of the situation and that if my father had still been fit and healthy things would have been completely different. Yes, indeed! So she could dominate me even more, control every aspect of my life, and play 'family life' on her own terms. In the end, she ended up with nothing except a family life in total shambles. I am sure she thought that I was going to come back to her again and make things up again like in one of her favourite soaps 'Sons and Daughters.' She must have been clinging to that idea until the end. This would have been such good news to bring to her fans telling them that I had finally grown up. I knew what she meant by 'grown up': basically abdicating any integrity I had left by letting her control every aspect of my life, even expecting me to stop mumbling when she searched my pockets after a night out to see how much money I had spent. When I did complain about it, she said that it was hers anyway. In retrospect, it is sometimes difficult to believe that this sad creature imagined that I was going to keep up this comedy eternally just to please her. How hateful and sadistic it was to expect that from anyone and, at the same time, to expect him to keep smiling.

After her death, it amazed me to hear from some of her closest friends that the main reason why people respected her was because of my father. From her nephew, I learned that, when she was young, there had been rumours she stole in people's homes while cleaning and other less fine things. It is possible that he said that out of spite after learning from the will that he was going to end up with nothing. Yet there must have been some grain of truth in it. This is not a wishful attempt on my part to help me understand her mistrust or obsession about her belongings; it is because it was just too extreme and never made me feel comfortable in what was supposed to be my home. Besides, why was she supposed to have lived like a saint when she was young? Anyway, it is all over now; may her soul rest in peace. People should stop all of this reverence we bestow on parents. Some parents are not even worth the name.

On the day we buried our mother, we went to visit my father at the hospital. Upon arriving there, he passed away and we were devastated to realise that we had to make more funeral arrangements. At his funeral, I met his daughter from his first marriage for the first time. I knew he had one, but my father had not seen her since she was a child. She told me that her mother, his first wife, had out of hate destroyed every picture of him and asked us if we could give her some. I was struck by the likeness of her children to my father when he was young and could not take my eyes off them in church. We did not get to talk and I have never seen them again. His death upset me but, at the same time, I also felt relieved it was all over. At least, I thought, he got his dignity back. He would not have to wear a diaper anymore. I sometimes had to help the nurse to restrain him while she changed his diaper. Nowadays everyone speaks about Alzheimer's, but it in those days it was barely spoken of. It is a hateful and nihilistic disease. I really hope that, should I ever come to suffer the same fate as my father, someone would have the decency to put an end to my suffering.

He was my father. The only one I ever had, and unquestionably one of the few persons from whom I received so much love and affection. I still feel guilty about the way I laughed with a so-called friend when my father asked this young lad the same questions time and again. Typical of people suffering from Alzheimer's, he forgot things and repeated the same questions time and again. In fact, I did not laugh because I found it was funny. I laughed, as happens sometimes, because I thought it was the only thing to do. My father did this also to another friend a guy called Eddy van Moer, but my friend kept answering him politely without showing any irritation. He would be surprised should he ever read this, but, only because of that, I still admire him to this day.

On the other hand, I would have hated my father to death had he sent me to school in this backward town and made me a part of life there knowing that civilisation was just a short distance away. It would have been criminal doing this, knowing that it takes only 20 minutes by car to get to Brussels. Surely, not even Belgium's world renowned pervert couple, Marc Dutroux and Michèle Martin, would inflict this kind of treatment on their own children. Life among Flemings would have been a real purgatory and a daily torture compared to anything I experienced until then. I wonder what would have been left of me mentally, or if I would have survived it at all. I shudder at the idea that some adopted black children might have known such a fate. Such things should be forbidden by law!

I still try to learn more about my father. When I look at the pictures of him on the Internet, it is sometimes difficult to believe that this is the same man I crept into bed with as a little boy when I was scared at night and who had been such a reassuring presence for me as a kid. He played at KV Mechelen his entire career, later going on to coach several other football clubs, such as Ostend, La Louvière and Patro Eisden. It was of the latter he seemed to have the fondest memories. Now imagine just for one second, me with my dreadlocks telling a complete stranger that my father was a former captain of the Belgian national team and the first player of KV Mechelen to be selected for the Belgian national team. Who on earth would believe me? I think they might not put me in observation this time, but lock me up for good instead. Most people in this town knew that my father was a former Red Devil, there was memorabilia all over the place in his house; but I rarely talked about it with Walloons. One day as a teenager, I went with two francophone friends to a bookshop in the City 2, a shopping mall in the centre of Brussels. There was a book about the history of the Red Devils; my parents had the same book at home. In it was a full page with the composition of the team that went to the first world cup in Montevideo (Uruguay). When I pointed with my finger to the man in the middle and said 'that's my father,' they both started to laugh their heads off. They never believed it.

I wrote to some of these clubs to ask if perhaps they had some old pictures of my father, but I never received an answer. I had heard about an old documentary in VHS format on the Red Devils that retraces the entire history of the Red Devils from their first World Cup in Montevideo up to the present day. Since it was no longer available, I wrote to the producer of the documentary to ask them if it would be possible to buy any old copies from their archives. Sadly, I never received an answer. I lost all memorabilia of him as well as all my family albums in the saddest and stupidest way imaginable. When we moved to Brussels, we kept all of our stuff in a storage box. Contrary to Bruno, I wanted to keep the bare minimum and get rid of all the other stuff instead of keeping everything in a storage box. Always behind with our rent, we neglected several demands for payment. One day, without prior warning, the bailiffs decided to remove our possessions and emptied the box. They threw everything away. I will never forgive Bruno for that. Anyway, we do not see each other much anymore.

Especially where Flemings are concerned, I do have serious misgivings about all these people who allow themselves to be carried away by their humanity and want to adopt a child of ethnic origin. Why would someone in his right mind consciously want to uproot a child born in Africa, Asia, or another continent and raise it in a god-forsaken place somewhere in Flanders where he would, in all likelihood, be alienated and bullied? Then traumatize it even further by imposing as a mother tongue such a hateful and inferior language that no one speaks correctly. Not to have thought this through is quite foolish; as if it was enough to haul someone from the gutter. Even though I adored my father as well as my mother before becoming an adult, I am not really in favour of interracial adoptions.

41

Growing up, there are certain things I would only have been able to discuss with someone from the same ethnic background, just as girls can only discuss certain topics with their mum. In Britain, it is almost impossible to adopt a child from another ethnic background. Although they intend to change the law by the time I write this book, I think that is the right approach. Besides, Flemings should not be allowed to adopt children of any other ethnic origin but rather stick to their own. The world this little kid will be ushered into is implacable. Flemings are probably one of the most racist species of the modern world. Considering their strong racist nature and their unbridled hate directed towards the Walloons, I think it easy for anyone to guess what is in store for a black kid. Welcome to the Flemish world!

The main question is: why choose to adopt a black child anyway? Is it because of a trend inspired by the rich and famous? I just hate the way all these little black kids get objectified by the rich and famous as the latest 'must have' things, like some designer accessory. It has even started to be trendy in Flanders with all the BVs (*Bekende Vlamingen*/Famous Flemish) posing with their adopted children in magazines. There is a journalist who had her own column called *"Diary of an Adoption"* with a picture of her and her exotic pet, a little black boy from Ethiopia, sitting on her lap in a Flemish newspaper called '*Het laatste Nieuws*' (literally means 'The Latest News'), in which every Wednesday people could read her experiences with her adopted kid. Amongst other things, she vividly describes how once he got so terrified when a family member came to visit him that he stayed on her lap for more than an hour in an apparent attempt to hide, the way he reacted when he saw snow for the first time and things like that. This experience with snow seemed to have disappointed her a bit because she expected that he would have reacted a bit more enthusiastically to it. In her articles, she sometimes refer to her adopted kid as 'our little blacky.' Her column ran for almost a year. The impression I had by reading her diary was that she was rather talking about an exotic animal that she was not sure how to feed yet. Then, there was another famous Flemish personality, coincidently also a journalist, who received even more press coverage after she tried in a documentary, 'The Mother of my Kid,' to retrace the roots of her adopted kid to a desolate place somewhere in Kenya with her in the middle as 'the great saviour.'

One question I asked myself by seeing this is: did these people ever come in contact with people from foreign backgrounds at all before deciding to adopt something exotic? Do they have any cultural links to black people? Another thing that strikes me is that it is mostly girls that get adopted, which is not a coincidence. Most prospective parents prefer to adopt a little girl instead of a boy. I think anyone could guess why. I heard of one adoption agency that stopped divulging information regarding whether it was a boy or a girl to prospective adopters. And why does it need to be a black kid? Or could it be that, on the scale of misery, a black child still appeals more to white people than one of their own kind? Following the earthquake in Haiti, I was taken aback by the religious zeal of so many white people wanting to adopt a little black, whilst there are so many other kids who need just as much help and affection closer to home. Or maybe did those kids come cheaper, and getting them was like running for the best deal.

I sometimes wonder what set of criteria and profile adopters need to comply to in order to become eligible. The whole thing gets too romanticized and glamorised nowadays. Some adoptive parents cannot resist seeing their humanity being put into the limelight. I think that without this recognition most adopters would die. Well, for that there is still no better place other than the telly. Normally, a person of colour is rarely seen on Flemish channels or the media in general, except when he is a footballer or a musician. For Haiti, however, it was time to make an exception and lift all those little black kids out of the anonymity. They got interviewed and taken care of as if they were little stars. Little kids are always far more interesting because they are cuddly and non-threatening. Oh, if only all these black men could stay like Webster or Arnold when they grew up! At least, earlier on, no one is distracted by this big thing so many people talk about that they may be carrying between their legs. Not at that age, anyway. As a matter of fact, my mother would have liked to watch this broadcast too. I could sense how that good feeling pervaded everything while a little kid spoke during a televised donation for Haiti about his relatives still left there, and how he tried to get in touch with them. All these BVs(*Bekende Vlamingen*/Famous Flemish) prancing around the set with only one worry on their minds: to be seen. Witnessing all this, it is hard not to want to fart - even if you don't have to - and puke, knowing that most of these sad bitches among the BVs would be the first to cross the street at night if they thought they saw one. By 'one,' I mean one that is not that cute any more, not little like Webster or Arnold, but instead happens to be, oh my god, a black man! Anyway, it is always nice to know that some of these sad bitches are so preoccupied with the well-being of the Negro, but it would even better to come over to my place and have some good time together. Fucking bitches!

The Flemings know that I am familiar with their prejudices. Upon entering a bus blindfolded, I could sense say whether I am among Flemish or Francophone people just because of the distinct excitement my presence would provoke. From the way Belgians look at me, I could say whether a person is Flemish or not. Even abroad, some Flemings find it hard to get rid of their natural backwardness. During my holiday in Morocco, from the airport to our hotel, a group of Flemish tourists were making all kinds of racist jokes on the bus about the people they saw through the window. I just could not believe what I was hearing. A black girlfriend of Bruno's had gone through a similar experience abroad. On arriving at the hotel, irritated by everything she had heard, she wished them in Flemish a good holiday. They were shocked and ashamed because they had not expected that *die zwete* (dialect for *zwart,* which means black) spoke Flemish. A few years later when I went to Thailand for the first time, I never thought in my wildest dreams that I would be confronted with words like *zwete* or *zwete Piet* (Black Peter) by Flemish tourists who did not have the slightest idea I understood them. They are such a bunch of hopeless peasants and probably always will be. Unlike the way French or British tourists do, when I see Belgians abroad I never try to seek contact with them but rather avoid them. My determination in doing so is even greater when I hear they are Flemings. I have never really managed to identify myself with these people or feel at ease in their presence. On top of that, Flemings still have to get used to hearing blacks speak Flemish, which makes avoiding any contact with them rather easy.

A cousin of mine from a black family works as a hired dancer. Whenever he has to do his act in a god-forsaken town somewhere in French-speaking areas, things go just fine. However, when he performs in Flanders, he knows beforehand that he will have to endure racist insults throughout the night. How does one explain that? An African friend of mine from the Ivory Coast came to live in Belgium as a teenager. He got married and lives in Waregem in the west of Flanders. He has dreadlocks and limps when he walks due to polio, which he contracted as a child. A sickness that could easily have been avoided if backward Africa would not associate vaccination with manipulation from western countries, evil spirits, and other stupid things, as is still the case in some parts of that continent. Well, despite the age of globalization and internet, his very presence still gets some people overexcited. Often this excitement is accompanied by racial abuse from the moment he gets out of the train station of his hometown and has to pass by groups of youths returning from their various schools. Yet he is a perfect example of a successful integration. He speaks Flemish with the particular accent of the people of this region, but all these efforts and the fact that he limps does not get him the least bit of empathy nor respect. I wonder whether Flemings are not genetically predisposed to be more racist than anyone else, and whether this has something to do with the specificity of the language. It is my firm conviction that this language contains some kind of venom that makes them behave like this. Anyone just has to observe the behaviour of cobras once they wriggle out of their eggs and witness their innate aggressiveness. The way they try to bite everyone is quite astonishing. Why could it not be the same with Flemings?

I once lived in a friend's apartment in Antwerp for some time, not far from the Central station. One day, I read in a local newspaper that, in the cafe of *The Zuiderpershuis* (a cultural centre), they had added a new terrace that made the whole place look like a little garden inside. *The Zuiderpershuis* is arguably one of the most prestigious places in Belgium for anything related to multicultural music. Just a look on their website at all the upcoming concerts says enough about how prestigious this place is. So I thought:

"Why not pay a visit?" Upon arriving there, I got a bit confused because a stand advertising upcoming concerts had been placed at the entrance of the cafe by some kids, hence obstructing it. At first I thought it was closed. A parent of one of the kids excused himself and placed it back where it belonged. While I was taking a look at the posters, all of a sudden, these kids started to focus their attention on me; then started to say all kinds of things to me, growing continuously louder and vicious. I stood there shocked. To frustrate their little pleasure, I grabbed my bike and went away. Unfortunately, it did not end there. Out of frustration, I guess, they did it this time for the whole street to hear. It made me feel so embarrassed that I hoped that a young girl sitting at the balcony of her nearby apartment had not heard any of it. I do not think there is any need to blame parents for that. As I said, it may be more of a question of genetics link to that venom that resides in their language.

The first year after the death of my parents, it felt odd living alone in this house surrounded by all their belongings. With Bruno away at university during the week, things could be pretty frightening at night. I still feel a bit embarrassed to admit that. Probably even more embarrassing is to admit that there were moments I felt so lonely and isolated that I called these sex adverts in the newspaper just to have someone to talk to. It took years before I got more or less used to that eeriness at night. The fact is once I went to my room on the third floor at night, I did not come downstairs any more. One evening, friends dropped me at my door after a reggae concert by the group Culture. I do not know why, but, while opening the door, I

46

looked instinctively up at the window on the second floor and thought I saw someone in a white nightgown. I was so terrified that, once inside, I did not dare to go upstairs and slept in the living room. I am sure that for most people this eeriness would have been unbearable. If I had not been so determined to not let my fears take hold of me, I would probably have gone mad in this house. My best friend ever, a Moroccan guy from Brussels called Abdel, asked me once after much hesitation whether I was not scared at night. By that time, I was already used to it, but what particularly struck me was that he of all people would ask me that. Like most Moroccans, he was rather the macho type and had one of these big motor bikes which he liked to drive around at full speed like a daredevil. We went together on his bike to many places, the most memorable being the island of Renesse in Holland. To get there we had had to cross the Zeelandbrug which at the time was the longest bridge in Europe. The island looked to me as if it had come straight out of a fairy-tale. It was a place worth to discover.

It took eight years before I finally quit this town for good. Bruno did not agree on selling the house, and the solicitor made it clear that as long as he did not agree, it was pointless to try. So there I was with my hands tied. The breakthrough came nine years later during my second stint as a handyman at the care home. I met some old colleagues, and we brought up some fun memories. Like how on one occasion the director, whom everyone thought was gay, had caught me with some porn magazines. On another occasion, which apparently no one seemed to have forgotten, I had been taking a bath in the middle of the afternoon in a friend's flat on the grounds of the OCMW. Completely unbeknownst to me, this guy had obtained some washing powder from the laundry room and put it in the bath while I thought it was just bath salts. This story made them laugh to tears. Fun memories. It was during this time spent with my former colleagues that one of them told me there was a way out of this joint property ownership deal and also told me of a lawyer I should consult. I did not believe it at first; it sounded too good to be true. Yet it turned out that he was right.

Finally, Bruno and I decided to sell the house to a construction company. Because of 'succession rights' we barely received anything. Succession rights are some kind of tax that some countries impose on inheritance. In Belgium there are among the highest compared to any other country that have them. The further down you are on the genealogical line of the family tree, the more you have to pay. Considering the fact that my brother and I were not even officially adopted, we had to pay back 80% of its original worth. I call it legally robbing people.

Selling this house symbolically severed any links I still had left with this town. I cannot describe how liberating it felt knowing that I was not going to grow old in this place and enable people to keep track of me anymore. The whole time I lived there, I always felt like an alien which maybe I was in some respects. I always had this feeling of being trapped there and under constant pressure. This town left me psychologically damaged and still haunts me to this day - as it probably will for the rest of my life. Except for my brother Bruno and I, this place had always been a negro-free environment when I grew up. I turned 27 years old before meeting another black person who came to live there. At first, there were mostly mixed couples; white men with black women. It began with a guy I knew vaguely who had been to Ghana and brought back in his luggage an African woman, thus preparing the way for some of his friends. On his second trip to Ghana he brought a friend with him. His friend, whose nickname was '*De Wannes*,' was a notorious drunk and quite a popular figure in this town.

"She will soon be coming," he had told people around him. "But I warn you guys, don't you try to lay your dirty fingers on her," he said while wagging his finger.

When she finally came, their relationship lasted just a few weeks. Yet things seemed to have gone off quite well at first. One day I met him, standing outside the pub of my godfather, and asked him how his wife was doing. "Oh fine," he said in his crude Flemish dialect, "she still looks as black as ever!"

Before I finally left this town, a whole African family had come to settle there. They did not stay for long though. Except the usual Moroccans and the Chinese from the 'Chinese take away,' the other people I saw from foreign backgrounds were from a much younger generation. Most of them were also adopted, but I never really saw them participate in any social activities around town. One adopted Indian I spoke with seemed to be the loneliest bloke on earth; I never saw him with any friends at all. Then again, who outside an Indian would find himself attracted to an Indian?

While living in Antwerp, I always hated having to comeback to this town. To wake up in the morning and being stuck there most of the day in the care home was extremely hard for me. It made me feel like an integral part of this town again, which was the last thing I wanted.

I had worked there under 'Article 60' - which is a temporary work contract that entitles someone to unemployment benefits if their contract does not get extended and it is also a fiscal perk for any employer willing to take on a social case like me. I left the job with other poignant memories. For instance, one day I had found a mattress in the garage and put it on the floor of the dressing room so I could have a nap whenever I felt like it. My colleagues would try to scare me by knocking on the door or imitating the voice of the director, which would always make me jump up from my mattress.

Except for people from my immediate surroundings, most people thought that I had moved away. Concerning Bruno, there were even fewer doubts. A shop owner even knew enough to tell where exactly he had moved to in Brussels when I entered his shop. I had lost all contact with those I had once befriended there, and I always hated to meet old acquaintances in the street, wanting to stop and have a little chat with me. Generally, I only came in contact with people from Brussels. Besides, there was another thing I was quickly made aware of in such a backward town. As an adult, I could barely befriend someone without people suspecting that there was something more to it than just friendship, even if they had already seen me with some girls. It did not really matter whether or not I had the slightest contact with these sad people, I was always part of their fantasies.

Chapter 4

Sister my sister

At the turn of the century, I finally moved to Brussels where at first I stayed at the house of an aunt. Actually, she was a cousin of my biological mother. She was not really the first person I met when I came in contact with other siblings. This arrangement had come about via the Congolese embassy, which is the only thing I remember. I must have been about fifteen years old. Bruno and I had to wait in another room and, on my mother's signal, go together to the living room where a sister of my biological mother, my Aunt Charlotte, was sitting with someone from the Congolese embassy. There was a lot of crying, mostly on the part of my aunt, and we received pictures of other siblings and my biological parents. Apparently, I had another brother and three sisters. Over the years I met more and more members of the family. However, it took more than a decade to meet some of them. I have a sister living in Tottenham who I still haven't seen. My younger brother, Max, was born in London where he still lives and my eldest sister Doudou lives in Rio de Janeiro. The truth is that I am not so sure whether this was the first attempt at contact from biological family because around that same period, I remember to have received a letter from Italy of one of my sisters asking for money. She pretended to be stuck there and that she was in urgent need for help. The problem is that I cannot longer recall whether this took place before or after this 'reunion' came up. Anyway, my parents were right not to pay attention to her demand.

I went to visit my eldest sister Doudou in Brazil just before the turn of the century. She came to live there with her husband whom she had met in Angola. I did not stay at her home but with some friends of hers. They lived in Barra da Tijuca, just fifteen minutes from the Copacabana. What more could I ask for? I stayed there for one month and lived like in some kind of dream. For a guy like me

51

obsessed with bubble arses, this was an awesome place to be in. Basically it was like some kind of arse-paradise, and I certainly got my fair share of it. The Copacabana is quite a surreal place for anyone who goes there for the first time. It is acceptable for women to prance their arse around in a string, but forbidden for them to go about bare-chested. Another thing most people would never dare to admit despite all the hype surrounding this mythical beach: it is one of the dirtiest beaches I had ever seen. Quite disgusting really! There was no real need to go to the Sambodrome to enjoy carnival for it was everywhere. I even did some paragliding. This was not the first time I travelled though. I had already been to Ibiza, Italy, Portugal, Morocco, Turkey and Poland. My trip to Poznan in Poland has been by far one of the craziest adventures of my life. By crossing the border to go there, I had been hiding under our luggage behind the back of my friend's jeep, a Flemish guy from my town. I was still a Congolese citizen then, and I did not want to go through all the administrative procedures required for a visa to go there. The year was 1994, and a country such as Poland barely got mentioned in the media. We were three young lads and stayed for at least ten days. Everywhere we went, we were looked at as curiosities and were even invited to sleep at people homes; only once did we have to go to a hostel. I still remember how weird it was looking at these Poles turned wild while listening to Rage against the Machine in the Jeep. We didn't know that this music was so popular in a country such as Poland. Besides, who on earth would have gone there? I could never have imagined that these brave people, who once, without any sense of ridicule, attacked German tanks on horses during the Second World War, would come en mass to Belgium one day.

People do not seem to get enough of these sob stories, like you see on the telly in which people get reunited and tears flow endlessly. I am afraid reality might be a bit different. For starters, I never really longed to see them and for all I know, some of them had never longed to see me either. In 2003, I learned that my biological father had died and that they were going to organize a wake in his honour in my aunt's home in Brussels. Did I give a shit about it! Why should I care about someone I never saw? He died a broken man, but I was told that he had been a quite successful businessman during his heyday. There could be a grain of truth in that. In those days, not every Congolese could afford to come to Belgium or go to London. This was something reserved for the elite. Had he already come to Belgium before he abandoned us at this nursery? I never knew. I guess he must have been one of those Congolese that liked to live beyond their means and show off as much as they could without caring much about the next day. It is quite a familiar story around the Congolese community. Shortly after the death of my white parents, I received a letter addressed to the name Lukemba George. I shared the same first name as my biological father. Later I received an African first name: Kelani. I think this had to do with the campaign of *authenticité* in which Mobutu asked every Congolese citizen to adopt an African first name instead of a Christian one. By the way, I never stuck to that Christian first name. I have used a lot of aliases - among them Glen, Ebory, and Gauthier - until I finally decided to stick with Gelindo. The letter was about a still unpaid bill that amounted to a half a million Belgian francs. It was left to me to convince the authorities that I knew nothing of his whereabouts, and that he had probably never again set foot on the territory since he left. I still wonder why it took these clowns so long to act.

The only one of the whole pack of sisters and brothers I really enjoyed meeting was my little sister Valèrie. She had come to Belgium in the late nineties from Angola, where she had been living with my biological mother and the rest of the family. My black mother went to live in Angola after her divorce from my father. Valèrie lived in Verviers, close to the German border. Yet it took two years before any of us really bothered to see each other. I needed to braid my hair, and I never liked to go to a hair salon for that but rather to a girlfriend or family. There were always many women at hand to do that - and at a fairer price, sometimes even for free. Before I went to visit her, I had been warned. "You will see," my biological family told me, "She is as crazy as you are."

You do not get far in Belgium without an ID card and for that you need a legal address. Once you have found somewhere to live - even if the address is only temporary - you have to visit your local town hall register and get your ID card or any valid document. Most Congolese who could not find a place to get registered in Brussels and its surrounding towns went to Verviers, which was apparently known for being less stringent about signing you in. Congolese, known for their strong personalities, went there in droves and had formed a little African diaspora of their own in a short space of time. It is a city 109 kilometres from Brussels, so to have to go there is like being exiled to the gulags. It is a quiet, provincial city. Yet, as I later found out, my sister managed to make it quite an exciting place all on her own. When I approached an African woman about the address my sister had given me - she had written it down incorrectly, quite typical of Congolese people! - I was bemused by the assured manner in which she explained to me where she actually lived. She did not seem to need to think twice about it. She was a much older woman and could not likely have been a friend of hers. I discovered, however, that everyone knew Valèrie in the African community.

When we finally met each other, it would be an outright lie to describe scenes of intense emotions, cries, or any of that shit. In fact, she had been peering through the window when I rang at her door. Since no one came to open it, I had enter a pharmacy in the neighbourhood to ask whether this was a correct address. She had been watching all this then came onto the balcony to shout and gesticulate that I had been ringing at the right door. For some reason she seemed still upset that I had gone into this pharmacy to ask for more information. "Why did you need to you go to this pharmacy!" was one of the first things she asked when I entered her living room. Sadly, I have to admit that she was not one of the most refined women I had ever met. After she cooled down a bit, we hugged, held each other tightly for a while and then life goes on, I guess.

Her skin was fairer than in the pictures I had received when she lived in Angola. Like many African women, she liked to bleach it.

However, this did not mean that she wanted to turn white. Similarly, when a black person wants a nose job, it does not mean he is especially looking for a Caucasian type of nose. He may just want to reduce its size a bit, like I would; I hate my nose. Some like Wacko Jacko even choose to have no nose at all. I never really liked African women safe for those assets more precisely those bums, that seem quite unique about our women. I found my sister was quite beautiful. I also came to meet her two lovely little daughters, who seemed to call every man they met '*tonton*' (Uncle). Later that night, I met Leo at a disco. His woman, my Aunt Adèle, was a sister of my biological mother. He was quite a character and liked to have a drink. At first, whenever I came to Verviers, it would be to pay them a visit.

There was a time when my uncle Leo used to express his *joie de vivre* by beating my Aunt Adèle from time to time; it was all part of his enthusiasm and his zest for life. This caused such an outcry in my black family that my uncle Omar, who lived in France, came all the way down from France, picking up Bruno in Brussels along the way to fix this problem once and for all. The ensuing scene was one of total humiliation for my uncle Leo. Bruno later told me that he just stayed at the window, too petrified to come downstairs to open the door. This must have been quite a scene, a middle-aged man too scared to move, just staying there at the window. So Bruno and my uncle Omar had to talk him into coming downstairs to open this damn door. When they finally got in, Bruno had to restrain my uncle Omar who would probably have beaten him into a pulp if he had not been there. My uncle had not come that far to have a little chat; he was not the kind of man for such things. He was an adventurer and a bit of crazy guy; quite a lot of people were scared of him. In order to survive, he had once been reduced in life to washing dead bodies in Egypt. One can rest assured that my uncle Leo never laid hands on my Aunt again. I told my uncle that I would pay them a visit before I left again. When we came back that night, there had been a parade of men trying to entice my sister, Congolese style, to go with them to Paris for the concert of Koffi Olomide, offering to take care of everything. Koffi Olomide is unquestionably the most famous

Congolese singer in the world. For some reason she finally decided on Major, her regular boyfriend who was not even there that night.

It was not the first time I would see Koffi Olomide. I had already seen him during the festival Open Tropen in Brasschaat (Antwerp), one of the first festivals during the summer in Belgium. Despite being such a nice festival, it often got spoiled due to bad weather. At the time, however, the weather had been fair, and his concert was one of the highlights of the day, well, for me anyway. In a nearby town where I went to eat, people crossed the street at the sight of me and a little girl started to cry when she saw me approaching. Sure enough I was among the Flemings. On my way back, a guy spontaneously offered me a lift. It was Pico Michiels! That was his stage name. He played in one of the most famous sitcoms at the time in Flanders: FC De Kampioenen. My mother enjoyed this sitcom. I pretended that I did not recognize him from the telly. I do not remember the language in which we communicated with each other. He told me that he had come to join his brother who was a DJ and was going to take care of the party that night. Gosh, little did I know that this lad was a total drunk! He had a fierce row about it with his girlfriend in the car; they did not even bother to acknowledge my presence. Years later, I came across this guy again by zapping on the telly, but things had dramatically changed by then: he had spent some time in a psychiatric asylum and could barely speak clearly because of his medication.

In the morning when I woke up, my sister was walking around in her string. "What an arse!" I thought. Had it been a book, I would have liked to open it up and turn the pages of it. I cannot think of a better way to trick people into buying more books. It took me totally aback though. Why on earth did she need to walk around like this! It made me think of a friend who told me how guilty he felt for having been sexually excited at seeing his sister naked in the bathroom. Happily, she did not have to bend over like they usually do, to pick up something that had been lying around. I wonder whether she noticed the way she aroused me, but then again, she could always have played her universal womanly role and acted surprised! I guess she would have said: "God, aren't you supposed to be my big brother!" They never seem to know anything, anyway.

Right then, she was just adjusting her wig in front of the mirror. Really, it was a pretty depressing sight, seeing our black women being reduced to wearing grotesque wigs, weaves, or whatever it is they put on their heads to look like *'femmes fatales.'* How sad! It is probably one of the most divisive, sensitive subjects among black women. In the black media, it does not take long to come across yet another article in which a black woman relates her experience with her 'new natural afro' and how good she feels about it now that she does not need to straighten her hair any more, or another saying how happy she is to have finally found a hair salon where people did not look down on her when she asked to have her hair straightened. I even read an article about a woman who said what a political statement it would be to see the wife of the President of the United States with an Angela Davis Hairdo. As hard as they try to pretend otherwise, these frustrations linked to the limited possibilities of their hair will stay with them throughout most of their lives. Every black man knows that. Actually, these deep-seated frustrations could be even more debilitating than any lack of orgasm. Maybe the best documentary showing to what lengths black women are prepared to go in order to have a bit of Caucasian hairstyle is the documentary of Chris Rock, the stand-up comedian. My opinion is that only a racist God could have been responsible for this. You fucking racist! Some of us, thanks to these lovely features of ours, cannot even deny Darwin's theory without looking like a fool.

Anyway, we were preparing ourselves to go to Paris. I had a feeling that this was going to be a big event! It was the first time an African artist managed to sell out at Bercy, one of the most prestigious concert halls in France. Everyone seemed to know about it. Upon entering one of the luxury designer shops, the shop owner asked us spontaneously whether we had come all the way from Belgium for the concert that night. By evening, the parking lot surrounding the concert hall was teeming with cars that seemed to

57

have come from all corners of Europe. I do not think I had ever seen so many black people at once, let alone in cars. The whole thing, the hectic atmosphere looked so weird to me. Well, I certainly enjoyed it. Early in the morning, I stayed at the apartment of my favourite Aunt, Marie-Jeanne, who was a sister of my biological mother, and the rest of the day we went shopping again around Paris. It is a simple fact that most Africans would rather starve themselves than not be able to buy trendy clothes; clothes are just an essential part of the way we are. There had once been a documentary about it on a Belgian francophone channel that received much debate in the Congolese community, but no-one really dared to complain of it being biased against us because it was damn accurate. As one African said: "when I'm dress well, I 'm not hungry anymore." My sister kept nagging her boyfriend for just about everything, especially for jewellery, as she had done throughout the previous day; it was never enough. One time, upon arriving in the African neighbourhood of Paris and entering a shop, it got just out of hand a bit. The shop owner, a beautiful black woman, was visibly shocked by what she saw and started to make me feel a bit embarrassed, too. So I tried to explain to her that my sister 'had just arrived in Europe.' This did not seem to justify it though.

"I don't know," she said, "but these people seem always so overexcited."

"My God," I thought, "she must have witnessed a few things about Africans in this neighbourhood." This was a black woman speaking after all, one that probably came from the French Caribbean. It does not matter how black they are, they have got nothing in common with Africans. She was not particularly light-skinned, but she had nice features and exuded style. When I told this anecdote to a friend of Bruno's, a Congolese lad, he laughed himself to tears. Not that he had any difficulty laughing, but seeing such a muscular lad laugh that way was quite a surprise.

When we finally got back to Verviers and I had some time alone with her, I witnessed some things that left me with no illusions. During the whole evening, people had been ringing at her door, and every time I looked discreetly through the window to see whom it could be, it seemed to be another bloke. She said they were friends, but that she was too tired to answer them and wanted to be on her own for a bit. The next day when I went to pay a visit at my aunt's, people started to talk. My Aunt Adèle begged me to try to change her lifestyle. She said that my sister was an embarrassment to the whole family, neglected her kids, and was considered a whore in the Congolese community. She also told me that my sister once tried to poke an old white man's eye out with a stick; a man they had found for a sham marriage in order to be granted permission to stay. Valèrie was in Belgium as a 'political refugee.' Her husband had been killed years ago in Angola. This event had completely changed her. However, these were very old stories. When I went to visit my other aunt, Aunt Charlotte, she confirmed the exact same thing: she was a whore! She shouted. My Aunt Charlotte, who originally came from Brussels, had come to live in this depressing city because of lower rents. The sad thing was that I could not even argue against it, things had been too obvious to me. As was to be expected, such a refined creature as my sister also needed someone to match her temperament, otherwise she would just have eaten him alive. She found the right match. Her boyfriend, a crook and the one she normally lived with, happened to be in jail when I came there. His speciality, like for most Congolese crooks, was dealing with credit card fraud, bounced checks, and fake documents used to falsely claim benefits. Congolese dealing in drugs are still rare. My family told me that her boyfriend had almost killed her once by trying to strangle her. Anyway, she never got permission to stay in Verviers and left for Ireland, where she still lives. For me, it was like the last thing that was missing on my CV: a sister as a working girl. Maybe I should not make too much out of that and rather show a bit of understanding, as Peter Sutcliff would have done with any working girl. Perhaps even derive some pride from it; it might be hip nowadays to have such a sister. The truth is that such an unstable, amoral creature could only have been but my sister. We were both the exact copies of each other: she did not shut up for one minute, was very impulsive and she knew it all.

Chapter 5

Oh La La La

I never managed to adjust to life in Belgium, or find work I could be passionate about. I always dreamed of working in the tourist industry. Not because I thought it would be such a dream job, as so many people like to describe it, but because I need more sun than anyone else. The first time I had a go at it was in 1996, before the explosion of Internet. I responded to an ad in a Flemish newspaper by Neckerman, a Swiss travel company. They were looking for animators. Initially, I was turned down but since I did not want to take 'no' for an answer, I sent my curriculum vitae again and finally got invited - as if they could not refuse me twice - to this big meeting that took place in a hotel in Antwerp. Upon entering the place, I thought that the whole event was going to be a boisterous and that I was going to be met by all kind of self-assured men, playboys - the kind you see doing kite surfing and stuff - and sexy chicks. It was none of that. The candidates seemed to have been chosen based rather on their lack of sexual appeal or, to be more precise, for not being sexually 'threatening' and conspicuous instead. I must have looked awkward in this place with my Milli Vanilli look. I was the only black person. What a surprise! Even these days when I sometimes visit their website, I do not come across any person of colour among the tour guides and animators. I had to present myself in front of everyone and explain what motivated me to want to work for them and shit. Afterwards, I had to pass an interview in the company of three people. I have always wondered whether their reasons for not recruiting me were not sexually motivated. Well, I certainly did not look inconspicuous, not to mention all the sexual fantasies surrounding black male sexuality.

Everyone knows that sex or your sexual orientation can be a determining factor in recruitment policies. To deny this would be hypocritical. It is generally known, for example, that most male flight attendants on Belgian airlines are gay. And if not, they certainly do not look all too manly. This trend is so common that when I went to New-York with Air Continental, I was amazed to be served on the plane by men who just looked like real men. With my effeminate hands, I am afraid I could not even be ranked among them. If those Belgian airlines had been more colour blind, I would certainly have fit the profile to work as a steward. I was also surprised to see black, not just light-skinned, flight attendants when I was walking around the airport in New York or at Heathrow. It is just baffling to see how some countries could be light years ahead compared to other countries while having basically the same percentage of people from foreign backgrounds. I spoke three languages fluently at the time, and they must have known that for someone who speaks Flemish fluently, I would have learned German in no time. During the interview they asked me if I knew someone who worked for their travel company. I told them about a girl with whom Bruno went to school at the College St. Pieter. Her mum came to pick up my brother every morning at our home. I would meet that girl a decade later at the club called 'The Mirano' in Brussels. That night, I also saw one of Belgian greats: Arno Hintjens, the former frontman of the band TC Matic who, as always, seemed to be in nice feminine company. He must be one of the few Flemish singers who appealed to the Francophone community as well. His sexual appetite was notorious. I was friends with a girl, a back-up singer, who knew him quite well. He was damn right! At least he was more alive than most people can claim to be at a far younger age. I think he must have been fifty-four or fifty-five years old by then. Little did I know then that we were born on the same day so I guess we might have a lot in common. Anyway, she told me she was still working for Neckerman which made me look at her with envy. I still wonder how my life might have turned out had I worked there. Would I still be in this backward town? It would certainly have made me happy to find myself in all those sunny places, all the situations one gets involved in, meeting lots of people. But the prospect of having to come back to this town would have been harrowing. Not that I had to of course, but the very thought of still having any links with this town or seeing it still mention on my passport would have been too much to bear. During that same period, I had also applied to other travel agencies, but nowhere did I encounter the same conditions as with Neckerman. The salary at Club Med, for example, was a farce. These people, who had been so pretentious in the past, were reduced to putting up big job ads in Employment agencies. However, meeting that girl that night inspired me to start all over again.

One morning, I was reading an article in a German newspaper *Die Zeit* about a holiday trip in Cape Verde organised by *Reisen mit Sinnen*. It was a rather nice coincidence because every day of the week, I would wake up early to watch RTP Africa on a Portuguese channel. I loved to watch this series because they spoke about countries rarely mentioned in the media like Angola, Mozambique, Cape Verde, et cetera. What I enjoyed watching most was anything about Cape Verde. This country appealed to me because it still looked unspoiled and because of all the beautiful women one saw in it. These were not just fantasies. During the summer, I had already come in contact with this community when I went to an open-air swimming pool in Antwerp. They had been organizing a barbecue in the surroundings. They are incredibly beautiful people, the women as well as the men. They may be Africans, but their skin seems fairer and their features are more refined than those of typical Negroes. Their women are unquestionably the most beautiful in the world! It was a joy, a real feast for the eyes, to observe how proud these women were to flash their bubble arses around and how their butt cheeks would wobble at every step they made. Watching such a spectacle, it is sometimes difficult not to believe in the existence of a God. White people will never understand this fascination for this. On the contrary, they seem to worship women for everything they do not have. Then again, who cares about what they think!

Spontaneously, I applied to the travel agency, *Reisen mit Sinnen* by sending an email with some pictures of my holiday in Salvador Bahia, inquiring whether by any chance they were looking for tour guides. A few days later, I received a reply that indeed they were, and they invited me for a *Vorstellunggespräch* (job interview). I still had more than a month to go and, as anyone could imagine, I was over the moon by this news. Although I had a very good understanding of this language and could easily express myself in German, before then I rarely had the opportunity to practice it on a regular basis. Two German lads I knew, one was from my tennis club and the other I met regularly in an Irish pub where I watched my favourite team - Manchester United - play, reassured me that I did not need to worry about my level of German. They both told me it was good enough for the job. It made me feel confident about myself. I cannot exactly recall the name of the town, but it was, like so many places in Germany, an utterly depressing one. I now guess this must have been an omen.

I arrived a day earlier in order to be on time for the meeting. I stayed at a youth hostel the night before. In the morning, I got a lift from two women who were also going to the meeting. I had not noticed them the day before, as I had spent the whole evening in my room reading my magazine, *Der Spiegel,* in a bid to practice on my German. The meeting took place in a chalet in the middle of the woods. We were one of the first ones to get there. From around 10 o'clock till 5 pm, I was thrown into all kinds of exercises, situations that could occur during my possible work as a tour guide. There was also an exercise in which I received a piece of paper with one word written on it. Then, I was asked to make up a whole story based on this word. There were other exercises like this. This was debilitating. It wore me out and, by the middle of the afternoon, I had lost any illusions about a future with this travel agency. I just wanted to go home. At the end of the day, when they were deliberating on who could stay on for the weekend and those who would have to go, I already knew what the verdict was going to be concerning me: I could go. As if I had not guessed that. The reason they gave for my dismissal was that my level of German was not up to the job. If only they had bothered to hear me out during a face-to-face interview, they might have changed their mind about it. There was not a direct train going back to Belgium so I had to stay in a youth hostel again, but this time in Köln.

I was devastated as I had invested so much hope in the dream of getting this job. I saw it as an opportunity that would completely revolutionize my life. Upon entering the dormitory, the only thing I had on my mind was sleep, but it was still early in the evening so I went downstairs to surf the Internet. There, I met a young Japanese lad from Brazil. He was part of this big community of Brazilian people with Japanese roots located in Sao Paulo. I had already heard about them. I do not even know whether they still speak Japanese. Anyway, talking Brazilian Portuguese with this lad lifted my morale a bit. Back upstairs, I chatted with some guys from Canada who were preparing themselves for a night out. I later regretted knowing exactly from where they came from. There are some things I did not want to discover about this country and will now sadly forever associate with it. When they came back that night, one of these lads let out a loud fart of the smelliest and fiercest kind: beer mixed with the smell of his bowels. He slept in the same row of beds as I did, which was close to the windows. There was quite a distance between his bed and mine, yet his fart got transported up to mine and beyond as if drawn by the windows that were open that night above each bed. I thought this was the end. The smell was disgusting and bewildering and made me even more depressed. I saw it like the icing on the cake and fitting perfectly with everything else I had endured that day. I had wasted so much money for nothing. Even though they were going to pay back half of the travel expenses, for me, it was still a lot.

Over the years, I tried again on several occasions, focusing not only on German travel companies but English and Dutch companies as well. I also took private courses in German. Anyone who finds work in Belgium and can prove that they have a work contract that is valid for more than six months is entitled to a bonus from the Employment office, good for sixty free hours of language courses either in Dutch, French, English or German. Due to my pornographic fascination with Hitler, I took German. Apart from that, it is also the language of one of my favourite film directors, Rainer Fassbinder, that of the ever-optimistic and smiling Schopenhauer, and of my absolute God and the greatest writer of all time, Leo Perutz. Most of all I had a strong desire to have a profound knowledge of this language with the aim of working one day as an unofficial translator. This language is so unpopular and despised by everyone that I thought there must be a niche for it. Yet despite all that, I still find German less repulsive than Flemish. With time, slowly but surely, my enthusiasm for wanting to work abroad for all of these foreign travel companies waned. There were some things I had never taken into account, the most important one was by far being my social flat.

I lived, and thankfully still do, in a nice social flat located in nice surroundings. I have been incredibly lucky with it. Every year the rent of social apartments is reviewed and based on anything a person earns in Belgium. This may even include jobless allowances, welfare checks, any kind of earnings. Someone who has a job has to pay far more rent than someone who hasn't. I do not know how the housing association would have reacted with nothing to base their calculations on. I had never put much thought into that until a close friend made me aware of it. The same could be said for my jobless benefits, and how this could have been jeopardized by working abroad for a foreign company if I then find myself jobless again. If this German company had hired me, honest to God, I do not think I would have given it much thought. My mind was too set on going, and my sense of adventure would have been too strong to resist. A year later, I called this company again asking whether they were still looking for tour guides. I was told that because of the economic crisis they were not looking for any tour-guides. Anyway, my salvation may well lie in writing.

I never fully realised how disconnected I was with Belgian society as a whole. Neither was I ever was much interested in exercising my citizen's right to vote for any political party and still have to see the inside of a ballot box. The reason being is because I never had a sense of belonging to this country and always felt disenfranchised.

Little did I care that this country went for so long without government due to the constant bickering between Fleming and Walloon politicians, or that Belgians were the butt of jokes all over the world because of it. It is not my country anyway. While abroad, I was constantly surprised that so many people knew about the political situation in Belgium. Some striking events that took place in Belgium I only came to know by watching foreign channels. On a Spanish channel, I heard this story about white couples that refused to be legally married by a black alderman at the City Hall of St. Niklaas in Flanders. However, what surprised me most was hearing about a black alderman. I had already heard of aldermen of Moroccan or Turkish backgrounds but never of a black one. Well, certainly not in Flanders. When I was young, the only foreigners I came across in this town were Moroccans. I remember to have gone there once to a nightclub with friends from my town; I was the only foreigner.

The alderman, Wouter van Bellingen, had also been adopted and was the only black alderman in the whole of Flanders, or probably in the whole of Belgium. I sometimes saw him from time to time while zapping on some Flemish channels, being the Negro at hand. One wonders how often he had the chance to see people of his own kind, or whether it flattered him when white people told him that he was no real foreigner anymore but 'one of us,' as I had to heard so many times. I do not think that his adoptive parents ever saw him as an African start with judging by the ridiculously Flemish name they gave him, Wouter. It is like having an Arab be called "Charles" or "Peter". They could have made it even more grotesque by giving him a German name like Wolfgang or Karl-Heinz.

Ironically, we had quite few things in common. His adopted family was pro-Flemish and were active members of the former ultra-nationalistic Flemish party, the Volksunie, which was the first political party vying for an independent Flanders. That in itself is not a big thing: the majority of the Flemish people want to be independent. But where it gets surreal is that this Negro, that is if he still sees himself that way, could somehow identify himself with this

67

cause as he explained in a Flemish newspaper. This sounded rather surreal to me.

"Who the fuck does he think he is?" I thought to myself. During a computer course in Brussels, I came to know a young lad from his hometown, a Moroccan called Abnnedour. This young lad, who knew him quite well from his days in the youth movements, told me that he seemed unable to identify himself with people from foreign backgrounds and that he actually seemed to despise them. I wondered whether, when in the company of white people, this Negro also points the finger at black people saying: "Hey look *ne zwete.*" He would not be the first one to do that. After all, his background, just as mine, has never been a very natural one and some people get totally de-naturalize.

The barman of my tennis club, also a black guy, told me that when he was young he once pointed with his finger to a black guy to warn his white friends about it. He grew up in Ruisbroeck, a town not far from Brussels where they were practically no blacks at all; but the irony is that he had not even been adopted. A friend of mine, a black guy, who had also been adopted, told me that he once said to his white girlfriend "hey, look a black guy!". "So what?" his girlfriend answered him, "You too are black." My own experiences are quite embarrassing too, to say the least. Maybe they were not as extreme as those of Adewale Akinnuoye-Agbaje (black British actor) who fought alongside skinheads beating up and chasing foreigners, but in a way they were as desperately sad: I laughed at black people just to please my white friends. It would not surprise me one bit to see this black alderman apply for the lead role of *'De witte van Sichem'* (popular Flemish movie about a blond kid from a village called Sichem) should they ever think about a remake and it might be politically-correct too.

My parents did not give a shit about this entire pro-Flemish thing, but most of those on my father's side of the family were active members of the same ultra-nationalistic party, the Volksunie. I, on the other hand, always felt ashamed to be considered a 'Fleming' by some of my Francophone friends due to my fluency in the Flemish language and always resented it.

68

It was by working as an employee at Smart, in Brussels, that I realised the degree to which I was alienated from everything. Smart is an organization that defends the rights of artists in any artistic endeavour by offering its members the same kind of social security network as those in a regular job. It is the biggest of its kind in Belgium. At Smart, they knew that I could not care less about my job. From the first day, I had made it very clear that I was only interested in my entitlement to jobless benefits again. My lack of subtlety is just too tragic for words. I worked there as an employee, again under Article 60, contracted for a year and a half.

It was the longest period I had ever worked. My attitude, or more precisely, my total indifference to what I was doing, must still be on some people's mind. My main task was to verify whether those who were subscribed to our organisation paid their fee in due time and, if not, to remind them by telephone; very passionate work indeed. It was supposed to be hip to work there. Well, I guess it was to a certain degree, but I could not care less. Having to stay that long at the same place, with the same people around me, is still one of the most gruelling experiences I've ever gone through. It still depresses me to see former colleagues just because of what they remind me of.

Any talk with colleagues about Belgian football, for example, was pointless. I just could not, which I did not particularly regret it. Who gives a damn about Belgian football when there are teams around like Barcelona, AC Milan, Manchester United, and Bayern München? It moved me sometimes to tears witnessing an entire police force being deployed to prevent any disturbances by Belgians 'wannabe hooligans'. What a waste of money and for what? A football league whose teams are barely known outside its borders? How more peasant-like can you get? Even as a son of a 'Red Devil,' I rarely watch a match of the Belgian national team. I have probably not done so in ages. It would be too agonizing, even for a bit of *schadenfreude*. It has never ceased to intrigue me how Belgians manage to be enthralled by their own football league.

The best reminder of that was when I came back to this backward town in 2004 to visit a friend called Rheinstein. I had called him at the library where he was the director to arrange our meeting. Going back to my town had been an emotional rollercoaster for all the wrong reasons. Yet I barely looked at the house where I had spent a great deal of my life. It had completely changed. I could barely believe it had been only five years since I had left this town. It seemed more like decades ago. That night Champion's League football was on the menu: Barcelona versus Chelsea. The match in which Chelsea defender John Terry scored a controversial goal with his hand. My mate had a telly, but not in the mobile home where I slept in the coming days. He was not the type to watch football and must have found that too traumatizing. So I went to the bar of a local football club. While I was salivating for the match to begin, all of a sudden the bartender changed the channel to watch a live match from the Belgium league! I just could not believe it and started to argue with him. He said that most people came to see this match and that I should respect that. Where on earth was I! I thought. I left still irritated trying to find a pub where they would show it, but it was the same thing in two other pubs I came across when I looked discreetly through the window. Then I went all the way to the pub of the godparents of Bruno, which was quite a distance away. It was full of people, but apparently for the same stupid match. However, this was not the only surprise. While I made sure that no one could see me from where I was standing, I was shocked by the interior. The place had not changed one bit! It still looked as old and as rustic as ever. It was the local pub of the football team where I played so many years ago as a kid. They had basically put wooden planks along the walls with a few tables and chairs and the obligatory bar stools at the bar. Probably their most famous item was their toilet without flushing water. It was basically a wooden plank with a hole in the middle. Even during my second stint as a handyman at the care home, a work colleague involved with this football club was still speaking about it. Yet these people, like so many in this region, were known to be filthy rich. I am talking about the Flemish region, probably one of the richest regions in the world.

I had barely recognised the godmother of Bruno from where I was standing. She had grown incredibly old. I had not seen her in ages. During the Christmas period, Bruno usually received three times more gifts than I did from my godparents, but they would always give me something too. I remember her daughter being a referee. She must have been one of the first female referees in Belgium to be in charge of a male football match. I wonder whether the players could keep their concentration. I once saw her in her referee outfit and thought: "Gosh, what an arse!" Although for white people such *rondeurs* might have been a bit too much to deal with. Though I was a child at the time, I will never forget how Bruno's godmother behaved just like a teenage fan when one of the absolute idols in Flanders came along for a cycling competition: Fons De Wolf. This man was worshipped like a God in those days! He had it all, talent and most of all good looks. I think he was still not fully professional and was being groomed to be a worthy successor to Eddy Merckx. Despite being a fully grown woman, she was unable to contain her excitement when she handed him flowers before the race started. Well, fully grown in my child's eyes anyway; she could still have been a young woman at the time. He did not seem to share her enthusiasm though. I still remember him coldly saying to her: "Gosh, what do you want me to do with these flowers?"

During that same period, I saw him again at another cycling event called '*De criterium*' which was a cycling competition held after the Tour de France in my town. This was a big event in those days. I had been there with friends of my parents and still remember being among a group of kids asking for an autograph. Among us was a much older girl; well, compared to us anyway. It was too obvious that she had caught his eye when he said to her: "I would like to see you again once the race is finish."

This girl was so awestruck that she could barely say anything. The last thing I heard about their great idol was that he was running a funeral parlour. I am sure that some people cannot help but notice some symbolism in that. After all, his career never really took off and seemed to have been nipped in the bud before it even started. One of

71

the few great cycling events he ever won was Milan-San Remo, but he was already in the twilight of his career by then. Then again, one must be criminal to consider anyone a worthy successor to one of the greatest sportsmen of all times.

During 'De criterium,' a family friend told me I should also keep watch on the cyclist in his green jersey, adding, "You will see why people call him the chameleon." And yes indeed, every time he came past us he would do all these strange things with his tongue, just like a chameleon. "Gosh what a freak!" I thought. His name was Freddy Maertens, one of cycling greats. He won the world championship two times.

I enjoyed my stay at my friend Rheinstein's mobile home. The whole thing, just being there, felt so *unheimlich* (German for 'surreal') to me, but at the same time I could not think of a better way to exorcise my past for having lived there so long against my will. At least now every time I took the bus to go back to Brussels, I knew that I was not obliged to comeback to this town in order to have a place to call home. I barely bump into any old acquaintances during my two weeks stay there, which made me quite happy. My friend had turned his two mobile homes into real pieces of art, befitting of someone who was passionate about art. People came to visit his mobile homes from all over the region. There was even an article dedicated to them in a French book about "hidden art" in Flanders. This did not help him to get settled though.

"They all (meaning the women) find it so beautiful, but not enough to actually come live here with me," he once told me.

Evenings, whenever we met each other, we would talk through the whole night. Life had not always been easy for him. He had once been reduced to working as a bin man, but now he was the director of the local library. How things could change! This guy had been a nice influence on me. As a teenager, I discovered through him the best reggae music has to offer. When I accompanied him and some of his friends for a weekend in the Ardennes, he introduced me to the reggae singer Linton Kwesi Johnson. He had a sound system, and organized parties everywhere. His music collection was like a hidden treasure to me. I may not love the Flemings that much, but oh God do they know something about music. I also went with him to the last punk festival called Seaside, in Veurne, where I saw Pil, the Ramones, Steelpulse, and others. We had gone there with a whole group of friends in a van. I still remember how creepy it felt looking through the window and seeing all these people around with their strange hairdos, coming from all over Belgium and beyond. It was also with him that I went to the weirdest underground concerts like Kiem, the Dutch punk band called the Ex, and Pere Ubu. It made me open my mind about music and not stick to one type of music as so many black people do. I know some blacks who feel bewildered when they do not hear any hip-hop. As much as I adore hip-hop, I also like to hear other styles of music without searching to viewed be as 'different,' 'integrated,' or 'westernised,' or having the need to act out as a faggot as some blacks do, who seem so confused about what they are. As if to say: "Look how artistic I am! Look at my white bohemian lifestyle! Look at what kind of faggot I have become!"

Chapter 6

Belgium has an appalling record among the countries of the EU for recruiting foreigners.
Joëlle Milquet

Trying to find work as a black guy in Belgium must be one of the most traumatic and debilitating experiences I ever have gone through. During a cultural program on a Dutch channel, Tom Lanoye, a Flemish writer from Antwerp was asked by the host: "How black is Belgium actually?"

He did not seem to understand the question. In fact, this host should have pushed him a bit and asked him: "Except footballers or musicians, are they also black cops, firemen, civil servants, journalists or columnists writing for the most popular newspapers in Belgium let alone in Antwerp?"

I do not think he would have needed much time to think about it. He could always have pretended of course, while knowing the answer from the beginning. Joëlle Milquet, Belgian Deputy prime minister for Employment and Equality admitted during an interview published by the Humo that Belgium has the worst record among the countries of the EU for recruiting people from foreign backgrounds. The Humo is one of the most popular magazine in Flanders especially among the youth. Blacks are barely integrated into the fabric of Belgian society and even less so in the Flemish region. I heard it is the country with the highest rate of unemployment among people from foreign backgrounds compared to any other country. The things Bruno and I had to go through during our job search were just an endless series of outright humiliations. It would be too massive to tell it all for it deserves a book of its own, so I will try to condense it as much as I can. Maybe the best way would be to start with the Belgian - especially that of the Fleming - public perception of black people. They still cannot get over the fact that a black person can do anything more than just play football or dance. It still baffles Flemings when a foreigner speaks Flemish as well as they do. At job interviews, the fact that I spoke Flemish so fluently was always an issue; for Walloon as well as for Flemings.

Concerning the latter, this is a bit ironic given their sensitivities and fanaticism about their language. Bearing in mind that some Flemish fanatics would disrupt any council meeting in a *'communes a facilité*' that takes place solely in French, or paint over road signs or street names written in French, even if they were written in Flemish as well; their watchdog called *'De Tak*' which is an organisation that would fanatically control whether the law concerning the Flemish language is implemented and respected at every public service place in Brussels, so that Flemish customers can be attended to in their own language; their big billboards with *'Waar Vlamingen thuis zijn*' ('Where Flemish are at Home') along the streets in Flemish towns; their yearly 'gordel' on bikes which can attract up to 60.000 people, with prominent Flemish politicians leading the procession. The whole meaning and political message of this event is to underline the Flemish identity of some Flemish towns around the periphery of Brussels and to reclaim it as such, much to the irritation of the Walloons living there. Their *'wooncode*' decree which gives the green light to any landlord of an apartment or house to refuse to rent or sell it to any Walloon who wants to come to live in a Flemish area in order to safeguard its Flemish identity. This decree has been condemned by the United Nations but nothing has changed since then. The local Brussels railway network (the STIB) banned French songs on their tube stations after some complaints from Flemish commuters. Yes, that is how far things have gone in order not bruise the *'amour propre*' of some Flemish fanatics.

The media is another big determining factor in the way Flemings perceive blacks or people from foreign backgrounds in general. We barely do exist in the Flemish media and when they speak about us we are rarely portrayed in a positive light. One is more likely to see a black face on a German channel than on a Flemish one. It took me a long time to get used seeing a black man with a woman of Turkish background present the news in the morning on ZDF, a German channel. Probably even more extreme was watching the television cook Nelson Müller, a Ghanaian who had also been adopted, showing Germans how to prepare some dishes. He did not have to act like a clown, but was allowed instead to bear himself with dignity. I have to admit that even I had my reservations about that at first. I judged it to be going a bit too far.

"What would Hitler have thought about that?" I wondered. "Have the Germans gone mad?" "Is there really nothing sacred anymore in this world?"

Here, if you ever see a black guy on any of these Flemish channels, it will preferably be somebody that gives them a good feeling, someone who laughs a lot or makes them laugh. Flemings are not used to black males or those from foreign backgrounds. They feel constantly threatened by them - especially black men who do not show them a lovely big smile - and the more they try to act cool, the more they look ridiculous. I never felt comfortable in their presence either. Besides, I cannot even imagine a black person being invited on one of these Flemish channels unless it was because he was black and this was relevant to the issue . The only time I see foreigners is during heated debates about racism or during dance competitions like "You Think You Can Dance" in which candidates compete alongside dancers from Holland. While zapping, it would be one of those rare moments when I saw many people from different backgrounds among the public as well. Unlike Dutch, English, or French channels, it is almost non-existent to notice a black face, let alone a foreigner, in the audience. It is such a rare event that, when it happens, it is worth recording it on your DVD.

The only time I saw foreigners living in Belgium being broadcast in a positive light was in a TV series called Couleur Locale from the nineties. Despite its French title, it was shown on a Flemish channel. The irony was that I was as taken aback as anyone else to hear people from foreign backgrounds speaking in clear Flemish about their daily life as migrants, the countries they came from and sense of alienation. It had nothing to do with the cliché migrant still struggling, after decades of life in Belgium, to express himself correctly - be it in French or Flemish as it sadly often the case. In my black family, there are still people who cannot speak correctly French after decades of living in Belgium. Well, this series lasted just one year. Except for the obvious lack of interest from Flemish people, I wonder whether Flemings could not bear to listen to 'foreigners' who, in some cases, were more articulate than them.

I heard that even the TV series 'The School of Lukaku,' about a multicultural Flemish school somewhere in Brussels attended by Romelu Lukaku, the young black football star, did not attract many viewers despite all the praise it received from the Flemish media. As someone responsible for the series said: "Flemings are just not interested in anything to do with foreigners speaking their own language."

The only time I ever saw a great many blacks at once on a Flemish channel was during a TV series called "Allez Allez Zimbabwe." It was a series about a cycling team made up of Africans from Zimbabwe. They were managed by Roger de Vlaeminck, a former great champion and Flanders great cyclist idol. I say Flanders because, although cycling is quite a popular sport in Belgium, he is barely known among the francophone public despite the fact he won four times Milan-San Remo. Africans who had demonstrated the potential to become fully professional cyclists in Zimbabwe were hoping, under the guidance of Roger de Vlaeminck, to further their careers in Europe. Although some of them had won trophies either in their countries of origin or in other African countries, this represented nothing outside Africa. But the public did not care, they had their fun. None of the Africans ever managed to reach the finish line during a cycling competition even at an amateur level, and were often the butt of jokes because of it.

To keep the public entertained, Roger de Vlaeminck also tried to convert them into cyclocross riders. It is a typical Flemish sport and one of the most popular in Flanders. Races typically take place in the autumn and winter and consist of many laps around a short course featuring pavement, wooded trails, grass, steep hills, and obstacles that require the rider to dismount quickly, carry the bike while navigating the obstruction, and remount. There is so little interest in this sport in *La Wallonie* or among the francophone public that I am not even sure they actually know it exists. It is a muddy event and comes to its fullest expression in bad weather. I have to admit how cruel this may sound that just as anyone else, I had tears in my eyes from laughing when I saw the Africans cycling through mud, covered in it from head to toe, and being barely able to move because of the cold weather. They usually abandoned the race after the first round. But, for the benefit for those watching at home, they were asked to cycle again through mud or pools of dirty water in front of the camera. This created surreal scenes and photogenic pictures. The public could not get enough of it. At its height, this series reach 1 million viewers from a population of 7 million Flemish.

Some Africans complained afterwards of having been exploited for not having received any money after this series was successfully sold to other foreign channels (It was never shown on any francophone channel). Well, I do not agree with their complaints. There had been constant problems with discipline in respecting a schedule for training, as was to be expected from Africans. They barely wanted to keep fit. The truth is that most of the Africans did not know what was happening to them. Life was just too beautiful. They were fed, hosted for free, and taken care of for everything. As celebrities they even enjoyed VIP status and were invited everywhere. Some of them - actually I think all of them - exploited their celebrity status to meet and marry some nice girls in order to be allowed to stay in the country. Afterwards, the women complained that they had had just married them for their papers. In some cases, from the moment they received the documents which allowed them to go back and forth to their home country, some of the Africans left their wives without caring the least about their new-born babies. Those typical things that are more common in black Africa.

Anyway, it does not really matter now whether they start to put some black faces on these Flemish channels or not. The lack of interest is mutual. One British euro MP, Nigel Farage, once described the Belgian President of the European Commission, Herman Van Rompuy, as having 'the charm of a dam rag'. Sadly, I look at most Flemings in the same way.

Due to my upbringing, it is indeed rare to meet black people of my generation who speak fluent Flemish; but this does not explain it all, and it would be absurd if it did. I guess there must always have been blacks who spoke Flemish, although they were more likely to be found in urban areas or major Flemish cities like Antwerp or Ghent. But even then there must have been very few of them and must have looked as if they got lost or stranded there given that the majority of blacks of my generation were to be found in Brussels and went to French speaking schools. In those days, it was unheard of for African parents sending their kids to a Flemish school because of the perceived inferiority of this language compared to French. I have never met a single black guy of my generation who speaks Flemish. That is how rare it is! It is quite new to see blacks and Moroccans going in droves to Flemish schools in Brussels. It has even been described as a phenomenon. This has mainly to do with the better standards of Flemish schools and the relentless drive by the Flemish authorities to make the Flemish language more popular in Brussels. Well, they have certainly the financial means to do.

The drive and energy in trying to achieve their goals can be compared to that of a Wahhabi movement. *'Het Huis van het Nederlands'* (the Centre for the Promotion of the Dutch Language) in the centre of Brussels gets assaulted every day by people wanting to learn Flemish. The great majority of the people who queue up there are foreigners sent by social organizations trying to win as many newcomers as possible to their cause. The Flemish authorities even intend to open one in Congo. Just because the Walloons already had a *'Centre culturel de la Wallonie'* there (Centre for the Promotion of the French Language) they want to have one of their own, too. How childish! As if we had no more pressing matters to deal with! I knew about this project through the President of the Flemish-Congolese organisation called Kuumba, who asked me if I would be interested to work there should this centre ever see the light of day. He may as

80

well have asked me whether I would be prepared to sell my soul to the devil.

Anyway, The President of the Flemish-Congolese organisation had far more pressing matters on his hands in trying to keep his own organization afloat. From day one, it had encountered financial problems. Their office, located in Brussels, had a place where people could eat, drink, and surf the internet, but I never saw anyone inside when I passed by. It was more closed than open. On the part of the Congolese, there just seems to have been no interest in it. I have to admit that for a language that has always been so despised in Brussels, I am still stunned by their success; I never thought it would be so devastating. It still surprises me to hear black teenagers jump from Flemish to French when talking to each other in tube stations or any other place. Once, when I heard two black kids in a supermarket in Brussels speaking only in Flemish to each other, it broke my heart. This was probably because Flemish was their sole language. It was like they had caved in to everything, saying hello to peasantry and having abdicated their dignity. I perceived it as some kind of triumph on the part of the Flemings. My attitude towards the Flemish language has changed a lot compared to when I was young; after all it is the language of the winner in Belgium. Yet I find it still heart broking to hear young Congolese or Africans in general having to struggle to speak correctly French or speaking it with a horrible Flemish accent like when I asked for the exact name of a street to young black lads at the train station in Mechelen.

Just as rare was seeing black families settling down in the suburbs of Brussels. Those who did often ended up being the only black family in town. This could even be the case for a such a big town like Meise, despite it being so close to the centre of Brussels. A Congolese friend of mine, Jean-Marie Kawende, was a musician quite well known in some circles. He even played before Queen Fabiola (Queen of Belgians from 1960 to 1993). Well, whether he really played before the Queen, as he never ceased to remind people, was doubtful. He did have a great picture of the Queen holding his hand, as if congratulating him, but this could have been for any special occasion. It was one of the first things he liked to show to anyone coming into his house. The truth is that he did not really need to because it was impossible to miss it. He settled in Meise with his wife and children in the nineties. They were the only black family in the town. Just a look at his face said enough what he went through at the time, starting with the daily harassment from cops. He did not really like to talk about it because, when he did, he started to get emotional. In a town where nothing ever happened, many of the young cops who wanted to see action frequently got an irresistible urge to arrest this black man in his car. It was as if the cops were taking turns in arresting him. He got so tired of it that he went on his own initiative to talk to the boss at the police station and told him that, if this did not stop, he was going to make a big case out of it thanks to his public profile. It worked, and he never got harassed again.

Nowadays, it is quite easy to hear people from Brussels, even foreigners, speak of having found an apartment in Meise, as if this were nothing. At that time, it was not rare to meet people from Brussels who had never heard of this town. Anyone would think it was a town on the other side of the world; often confounding Meise with Metz in France. Yet this town is now known all over Belgium for its botanic garden. Over the years, its outlook has completely changed. There are people from all kinds of backgrounds now, whereas just a little more than a decade ago, a foreigner, let alone a black man, was a rare sight. The town that has undergone perhaps the most extreme change must be the lovely Flemish town of Halle. Whenever I go there on my bike along the canal, I am constantly struck by the high number of black of people I see there. It is full of black kids mingling with whites and speaking Flemish to each other; they are everywhere, especially in the areas around the train station. I even saw black bus drivers! "Oh my God where is this town heading town to," I thought to myself.

Another thing that also struck me: its fast rising number of Moroccans. I am afraid that white people might be even less happy about this turn of events. Over the years, more and more Walloons came to settle in Halle, as they did with so many Flemish towns around the periphery of Brussels. This led to the Frenchification of some Flemish towns that were not necessarily « Communes à facilité », much to the dislike of the people living there. It is easy to guess how this causes tensions between these two culturally and politically distinct ethnic groups. Walloons have a totally different mentality than Flemings and often refuse to adapt or learn the Flemish language. So, everywhere they go, they want to be spoken to in French, as if they were in conquered territory. Walloons did not come to settle there because of cheaper rents, which could have been the case in the beginning but must now be a distant memory; they were fleeing the islamization of so many areas in Brussels (the great taboo in Belgium). The (real) Belgians have also a right to feel comfortable about the place they live in and to feel at home without being labelled racists from the moment they say so. The irony is that they were often trailed by the very people (the Arabs) they were trying to flee.

A Flemish woman living in Halle whose husband is Senegalese, once said to me with an air of disgust: "They (the Arabs) are all coming here!"

In 2001, Bruno worked as an engineer for T-Plan, a company for fiber optics in in this town. During lunchtime, when he went out for a place to buy something to eat and had to pass in front of a school, little kids got excited by his presence saying "Hé kijk een Neger!" (hey look a Negro!). At that time, Bruno told me, you didn't see any black at all. That is how rare the sight of a black person was in those days in Halle. I would be the first to understand if people from a younger generation, especially those living there, might have a hard time believing this. Anyway, they just need to ask people around them. There was a time people constantly asked me whether I was Dutch whenever I spoke Flemish. On my way to Cuba in 2009, a Flemish guy seating next to me on the plane likened my accent to the people in The Hague. Sadly, I never had the opportunity to find out what the accent of people from The Hague sounded like, or what set them so apart from the rest of the Netherlands.

Most Congolese of my generation were not born in this country and, in fact, came here to study. It was assumed that we would go back to our mother land once we finished our studies. Many of them overstayed their time like those, for example, who did not study anymore and no longer had any way to justify their stay in the country. This automatically created a lot of problems, which the cops knew all too well about. I grew up as part of a generation that lived in constant fear of being deported. The way cops used to harass us must have been worse than the 'Sus law' in England, which enabled police officers to stop and search members of the public even if they had no hard evidence that a crime had been committed. Every black lad of my generation has known this "stop and search" tactic by cops. Oh, those were jolly good times for cops, and so much fun, especially if you were stopped and searched where there were a lot of people around. The person had to lay his hands on top of the car and spread his legs while at the same time getting search for I-do not-know-what. This was a common sight in those days. In some cases, the fact that someone looked young or dressed stylishly did not matter; it was all part of the fun. This continued harassment only came to end after much protest from the public. Yet, having said that, I am afraid I cannot tell any tough stories about my encounter with cops. Despite having had to endure my fair share of harassment, sometimes even sheer humiliation, I never had any trouble with the law. My record must be as clean as the arse of porn actress Cherokee.

Perhaps the most surreal thing that ever happened to me with cops took place in Antwerp in 2006. I had taken a day off from work and chosen to go to a recreational park with an open air swimming pool at the Sint Ana beach area, in the centre of Antwerp. I thought this was going to be great fun for it was in the middle of the week and, with summer season already practically over, there would be fewer people around. At some point, I took my bike to drive outside the recreational park and just drove around wherever my fancy took me. This must have been quite a sight, this rasta man with his long dreadlocks in only his tight swimming trunks, certainly too much to resist for some cops driving around in their police van. So they

84

stopped me under the pretence that I had driven through a red light. Then, I was asked if I could prove whether the bike belonged to me and finally, without the irony of a Louis de Funès (French comic actor) chasing a bunch of nudists to ask their papers, they requested mine. I tried to explain to them that my papers were in the locker room at the swimming pool, but it was all to no avail. They ordered me to put my bike inside their police van and go with them to the police station of Zwijndrecht, which seemed to be quite a distance from where I was. Upon arriving at the police station, people just could not believe their eyes; cops as well as some onlookers. Needless to say that some of them could not refrain from laughing. I was still mad and could not stop shouting insults at them, as I had done while in their police van. It had nothing to do with my feeling in any way embarrassed being only in swimming trunks; otherwise, I would not have been cycling around like that through towns in the first place. I was annoyed at the sheer absurdity of the situation and waste of time. Still unsure about my real identity and everything I had told them, they drove me back to the swimming pool to have a closer look at my identity card. It frustrated them that everything I told them corresponded, and for that, they were going to make me pay: the whole farce cost me 250 euros for insulting a cop and driving through a red light.

In the nineties, as a young man, I went to the Employment Office in Brussels to look at some job ads. At that time, anyone who came across a job ad fitting his profile, had to write down its number on a paper and go with it to someone at hand for more information about the job. This one happened to be for a Flemish organization near the Madou underground tube station. Sadly, I have forgotten the name of this organisation.

"I warn you," said the employee before I left, "*Ce sont des flamingants*" (They are Flemish nationalists).

When I arrived there, I immediately noticed that the director of this organisation did not really know how to deal with me. He seemed a bit confused at first, panicked even. I could see him wondering aloud whether the term "migrant" applied also to blacks nowadays. It was a positive discrimination job ad, and the reason for his confusion was that, as such, he had rather expected a "real immigrant." A "real immigrant" in Belgium still means either a Moroccan or a Turk. It took years before they started to use the word "foreigner" for these types of job ads in order to include all people from foreign backgrounds. The same can be said of any program on the telly about how people from migrant backgrounds fare on the labour market. They would still rather focus their attention on the "real immigrants," as if we Congolese did not exist or were not bothered to work. This is quite ironic because, as a people who had been colonized by the Belgians, it is actually we who should be the recipient of any priorities and *traitement de faveur* instead of their "real immigrants." As a Congolese, whenever I saw mention in a positive discrimination job ad that they were encouraging people from migrant backgrounds to apply, I knew that it was worthless to even try. Anyway, after he got over his confusion, he tried to act as if everything was normal. He explained to me that his aim was to give any dropout with limited prospects in life another chance, and more of that romantic shit.

From the outset, the odds were stacked against me: I had gone there in a far too dignified way. My clothes were much too nice, my back much too straight when I walked, not to speak of my articulacy in the Flemish language. This was not the way a "social case" ought to behave himself. My entire manner must have looked provocative to him. Yet, for the purpose of maintaining appearances, I was invited for a second assessment. How can one forget this! They all sat there around a table - there must have been at least five of them - when I entered the room and said, *"Goede avond iedereen"* (good evening everyone). They responded in unison, *"Goeie avond,"* Insisting loudly on ignoring the "d." Actually, I still do not know which one of the two sentences is correct. These peasants were going to quibble now on such little things. From the moment I sat down, they started to fire their questions at me. Based on what they were asking, it made me think they were rather looking for an expert instead of some dropout. At one point, a man apparently got tired of speaking correct

Flemish. Pointing with his finger at the ceiling, he asked me in his dialect if I would be able to repair the plasterwork that had broken down in some places. This was absurd. Yet I replied that I was prepared to give it a go, but was not sure I could do it. The whole thing had been a grotesque farce. They had just invited me to keep themselves entertained and to reassure themselves that, in inviting me, they had been open-minded.

This has been my staple diet for most of my life: being invited for job interviews in order to entertain people and make them feel important and all-powerful. Having me to answer their imbecilic questions knowing that the whole thing will inevitably turned personal in an attempt to find out where I learnt to speak Flemish, how this came about, whether my parents were still here, if I had been adopted, did go to a Flemish school, and so on. Most of the time, they got frustrated because I would not satisfy their curiosity. Women especially were the most curious.

Still in 2002, when I went to register myself at Adecco (a recruitment agency) in Anderlecht, an employee, despite being busy with someone else, started to laugh out loud when I was asked whether I could speak Flemish and I answered in the affirmative. I did not say anything of course, for this could have been interpreted as being confrontational. For a long time, I had people calling me, especially young girls trying to make themselves interesting on the phone, just to hear me speak Flemish. A Walloon once laughed at Bruno over the phone for having mentioned on his CV that he spoke 'very good' Flemish.

"This must be a joke, mustn't it?" she asked.

I lack words to describe how this whole experience trying to find work demoralised me and left me dumbfounded. I am afraid to have seen too much. It is far more exciting for them to show a documentary with some naked Africans walking around with a penis sheath around their dicks or having, for entertainment on some Flemish channels, some Flemings sent to live among a tribe somewhere in Africa like in a Flemish successful reality-TV called "*Toast Kannibaal*." I think that the title of this series says enough. Just a look at their faces and their enthusiasm whenever they need to sign you into in any of these recruitment agencies speak volumes. In Brussels, most of the staff of these recruitment agencies is Flemish; which is understandable in a way for the language skills of francophone people in general is appalling. In my field, administration, it was indispensable to be fluent in Flemish or at least be bilingual. I always used to present myself in French when I entered one of these recruitment agencies. First thing they would ask with almost an air of defiance and a thick Flemish accent is:

"*Vous maîtrisez le Neerlandais?*"(Do you speak Flemish?). They would be frustrated by the fact I actually did and have to go through all the procedures to sign me in. Then I would call them time and again, but from their side, never receive a call. Eventually the whole thing died out like all the rest of them. It is common knowledge that when they need someone to fill in a vacancy, a black person is the last on the pecking order. First, would be the real Belgians, then those of European descent, then eventually Moroccans or Turks (their 'real immigrants') and lastly, if there is really no one left to choose from any more, blacks. Time and again, most of these recruitment agencies have been accused of racism.

This has also to be put in the context of continuing tensions, constant bickering between the Flemish and francophone communities. The accusations on the part of the Flemings about Walloons' supposed arrogance, lack of integration, and unwillingness to speak Flemish. Every Flemish politician who wants to score during elections, make a name for himself and be popular among his public, has to say something denigrating or insulting about the Walloon. Yves Leterme, one former prime minister once said that:

"Walloons are intellectually unfit to learn another language." This former prime minister knew a thing or two about what being "intellectually unfit" means. One day, for the fun of it, reporters asked him to sing the Belgian national anthem. Oblivious to ridicule, he sang 'La Marseillaise,' the French national anthem. In this tense political climate at the time between Flemings and Walloons in their desperate to form a government it had been the only common ground they had managed to reach by laughing their heads off without, for once, bickering with each other. It was not the first time that Yves Leterme caused some controversy with his disgusting remarks about the francophone people. He also once compared the francophone TV channel (RTBF) with the Rwandese Radio Mille Collines for its "unfair" portrayal of Flemish politicians and Flemish people in general. This radio was reputed to have led to the genocide of Tutsis in Rwanda by inciting racial hatred against this minority group.

In Brussels, the only sectors where one is likely to meet lots of people from foreign backgrounds are the cleaning industry, call centres, hospitals, and care homes. There has always been a chronic shortage of nurses and caretakers, and, with an ageing population at stake, there are going to be a lot of arses to be cleansed. For such things, there should still be a great future for us, albeit a smelly one. Practically all the women of my biological family work as nurses, either in care homes or at hospitals. The one exception is a cousin who works as a laboratory assistant. When she started working there, people asked her constantly whether she had been adopted

Bruno was not faring any better in his search for work at the time. We were both unemployed. He was so desperate at one stage that he wrote a letter to the Minister of Belgian Co-operation at the time (Réginald Morrels) to ask him for his backing when he applied and funnily enough, the Minister agreed to do so. I do not know any more about how this came about but I certainly remember how employers were desperate for construction engineers and how they spoke on the telly to make the career path more 'sexy' in order to attract more students to it. Of those with whom he finished class, he was the only one along with another foreign lad, a guy from Iran, who still had not found anything. At the time, students, prior to graduating, already received offers from various companies. He and this guy from Iran never received anything. This could also have been pure coincidence, of course. Stranger things happen. It just beggars belief what he had to go through just to be entitled to a job interview. If I had not witnessed this or had not had similar experiences myself,

I would never have believed it. I wonder whether he was not aware of that. He may have avoided one of the most acerbic persons on earth. Because that is what I am: an all-knowing type of guy of average intelligence with a lot of comments to make on just about anything. What happened in the end was that every time he applied for a position mentioning the name of the Minister in question as a reference, companies started to respond directly to this minister or, more precisely, to his staff. Then one day, the Minister's secretary called Bruno and asked him to stop mentioning the Minister's name. He had done enough now, she said. Enough was enough!

Previously, in order to obtain a job interview he used the name of our father (Hellemans). Every time he did this, we had to take turns manning the telephone. In the end, however, this also turned out to be a waste of time, as they impede his applications later. The only thing that must have frustrated them was to have wasted so much time in keeping up appearances. In such a backward country like Belgium, having a black guy as an engineer with high responsibilities was just too much too deal with. After initially working as a teacher at the Foyer, an alternative school in Brussels for young delinquents, he finally got a job as a construction engineer for a company in Ghent. He was lucky, as he was in danger of becoming side-tracked for ever. On the day this company was relocated to brand new office, they had invited Ms. Miet Smet, Minister of Employment at the time, to inaugurate the new premises. It was Bruno task to show her around and photos were taken that day. Their intention was to play the multi-racial card which was a sad joke as he was the only person from foreign background there

In the end, I got so frustrated from all these negative answers in my job search that I started to write back to all those from whom a received a negative answer. But, before sending them, I dip my letters into my own excrement making sure the whole thing was still readable. In other words: I started to throw with shit around. In these letters, I first started to speak out my mind then gave a few tips on how best to enjoy sniffing those brown spots on the paper. Then I suggested to bring them slowly on their nostrils or to cut them out and put them in hot water in order to brew a lovely tea out of them. Sadly, I never received any feedback on whether they followed my instructions correctly or how sweet it tasted. I fondly called these letters "caviar letters" and must be widely known by now for this campaign has lasted for quite some time.

One of the most 'prominent' public figures to receive one of "my caviar letters" must have been the head of the anti-racism movement; a Flemish priest called Pater Leman. He got the honour to receive more than one. I wonder whether he kept them as collectable items considering how sick these people are. I could not understand - and never understood - why a white person would voice his concern about discrimination on behalf of black people. I was alluding to his spokesperson at the time; as if we were too stupid to speak for ourselves. In every other country, in such organisations there are people from foreign backgrounds speaking on behalf of minorities except, of course, here in Belgium. Neither was I too pleased with seeing an emissary of a paedophile organisation namely the church, being at the head of such a movement. This is not cheap sensationalism; the church is by far the biggest congregation of paedophiles in the world and their priests the ultimate sexual delinquents. Yet in Belgium, there has not been one single case in which one of them was put into a mental asylum whilst there have been plenty of other people locked up and rotting away for years on end on far lesser charges. If anything, they always get protected by their own hierarchy and are not obliged, unlike other perverts, to follow a therapy. When things gets too hot for some priests, they are even sent by their own hierarchy on "catholic missions" in Africa or Asia where they can continue in total impunity to destroy the lives of innocent kids. The most notorious Belgian paedophile priest to have been sent on many such missions abroad must be Roger Vangheluwe, a Flemish priest. He is the Olivier O'Grady of Flanders, one of the most known paedophile priest in the world. Despite all the repulsion he provoked in this country, this Flemish priest does not seem at all perturbed by it. On the contrary, he find it quite amusing all the media attention around his person, minimizing what he did, almost laughing at all his victims including his nephew

Where else in the world would the head of an anti-racism movement be at the same time a "friend and close colleague of paedophiles?" And what about him? I would not go as far as to pretend he could be one but, given what we know about them, there is every likelihood of this being the case. I asked Pater Leman why whenever there was some controversy around race, he always needed to send this white person from his movement to speak on our behalf. Could he in any way relate to our problems? Did he go through the same experiences as we did? I asked. Another time, I also asked him to vigorously denounce all this hypocrisy in the NGO sector. This "close-friend-of-paedophiles" priest said very condescendingly, that beside the fact that there were quite a few foreigners working in his organisation, the best means of obtaining anything was still by being diplomatic. I must indeed admit that he once said in a Flemish newspaper that the NGO sector would certainly benefit from working with people of African-Belgian background, but this was in no way a condemnation of the sort I was expecting. Once, he also said that people should stop concentrating on terms like *gastarbeider* (guest worker) or "from migrant background" but rather use the word 'foreigner' in order to include people from all foreign backgrounds. It is needless to say that, whenever I tried to apply there, I received a reply the same day saying that my services were not required.

I guess that is why I so much admired Abou Jaja, the nationalist Arab leader of Flanders. Oddly enough, he is barely known in the French-speaking part of Belgium. His movement had nothing to do with the paternalistic organisation of this priest which he had often publicly criticized for its condescending manner. There was finally someone from the migrant community to voice their concerns. It did not bother me at all that he was only concerned about the needs of his people, the Muslims. Besides, I would not like an Arab to be speaking on behalf of black people. Arabs are not that fond of blacks anyway. The feeling is mutual. He was a sensation and sparked some controversy by claiming that the Arabic language should be considered the fourth language in Belgium. I do not think he really meant it when he said this; he was far too intelligent for that. At least however, it had the desired effect: it shocked people and enabled him to get himself into the limelight. He used that platform to get some of his more important messages through and point the finger at things that everyone would rather keep quiet about, acting as if there was nothing unusual. One of his main concerns was the blatant discrimination on the labour market. The one thing that the Belgians did not expect though, as happens so often, was that when he started a political party, it would grow so big. Well, certainly big enough to be perceived as a threat. So they started to criminalise him trying whichever way they could to kill him off politically, accusing him of just about anything they could throw at him. All this hysteria for just one lad was irrational. Some of the gravest accusations were quite cliché really, like his supposed links with terrorist organizations and the fact he manipulated disadvantaged young Muslims for his own ends, and, last but not least, for being a close associate of Bin Laden. They even found - oh dear! - paedophile material on his computer. People knew it was bullshit but liked to believe it.

One day, Bruno was playing football in Flanders with a team from Brussels. He was surprised to hear so many people talk about Abou Jaja. One woman shouted to her friend:

"Hey, they finally got him!" And yes they got him as the former prime minister , Guy Verhofstad, made sure that this was going to take place by legal means or not as he declared publicly.

There was also another anti-racist movement called Mrax. Its boss, Radouane Boulhal also an Arab, was even more media-hungry but at least pretended to be concerned by all forms of discrimination no matter the person's ethnicity; which was a farce based on the testimony of former disgruntled employees. In fact, he seemed only preoccupied with the needs of his own kind, the Muslims, as it probably was its original purpose. Some former members of this movement who quit in disgust had meanwhile formed another movement called 'SOS racism' insisting that they were there for everybody and not just to defend a certain people's identity. When a school decided to ban headscarves, this Arab could always be counted on to stage a virulent protest at the gates of the school in question. It is needless to say that his movement had also been accused once for being sponsored by 'terrorist organisations.'

Personally, I like these women to wear these headscarves because I know how much it pisses off the Belgians for it does not comply with their view of the world. One is tired of these sob stories about how these women are supposed to be 'oppressed.' If the Belgian people are so moved by justice and equality, why not extend this sentiment to all kinds of injustices and inequalities? Why not start imposing, for example, on all public places or workplaces a quota of people from foreign backgrounds, or highlight all kinds of discrimination with which we are faced on the labour market? Why do they seem only willing to move into action when it is about these poor 'oppressed women' with their headscarves! They seem quite obsessed by them; as if these veiled women had ever been as asking for their help, let alone their attention.

Another prominent figure to be the focus of one of my "caviar letters" was the Flemish director, Guido Gryseels, of the Royal Museum for central Africa in Tervuren. He too received more than one of my "caviar letters".

Anyone entering this museum finds it hard to get rid of the feeling of being thrust back in time to an era they seem rather nostalgic about. The whole place exudes something anachronistic, to begin with their grotesque statue in front of the museum of one of the greatest criminal's minds in history: that of Leopold II with his legendary trim stubble. This man was not less criminal and appalling than Hitler. It would be the same as having the Germans erect a statue or a street named in honour of Hitler. Why not, after all? He too did some good things for his people. Had Time Magazine not voted him 'Man of the year' when he came to power? If Hitler had not gone to war or lost it, he would probably still be considered as one of the greatest personalities to have ever lived. Come to think of it, this must be one of the first places I ever sent a CV to when I quit

94

school. This director was not even there yet. I had a close friend working there, Alberto Lopez. He was struck by the fact that there were so few blacks around among the staff while this being, after all, an African museum. Laughingly he told me that when he worked there, one of the few blacks around was a lad who distributed the post. In fact, he was more like their handyman. Nothing has changed much since then; one just needs to go onto their website and check their list of staff. The great majority of the names sound as Flemish as ever, with the exception of maybe one or two African names. During a night out with him, my friend Alberto met a former colleague who had also worked there. They were laughing their heads off when my friend brought up the subject about the lack of blacks working there; but what made them laugh even harder was the grotesque attempt of the museum to clean up its act. They (the museum) had apparently made a few changes. By far the most radical one was putting on their website an African in a white lab uniform looking through a microscope. The kind of docile Negro they must have been dreaming about. One that does not even need to drink or eat, and probably also did a lot of extra hours. In short, a good Negro; one that is educated but still knows his place in the world. Well, his docility did not save him because he is no longer to be seen on their website. Maybe he had suddenly started to speak and turned out to be quite opinionated. The fact is that I thought I could bring some change to that. I knew the director had a preference for Flemish people so I thought a Congolese sending a Flemish CV might do the trick. I applied for anything one can think of: for a vacancy as gardener, to sell tickets during expos, as a host for guided visits around the museum, for any administrative function, you name it. Not once did I get invited for a job interview. It got me so frustrated in the end that I wrote an email to him expressing my disappointment and asked him whether he did not find it a bit awkward to barely come across any African names on his list of staff. It was during the Christmas period of 2002. This must have broken a taboo to talk so openly about it and certainly did irk him. A few days later, I received a reply in which he said that there would never be any future for me in this museum. Over the years, I sent this arsehole hate mails, 'caviar letters,' postcards which would have won any competition for vileness from as far as Brazil and Cuba. Should I ever see this scumbag in person, I am afraid that I might find it difficult to control myself. I cannot think of a better illustration of a senile old white man stuck in time - the same can be said for his museum - and probably thinks that colonization is still going on. It is a view shared by many people; whites as well as blacks. Tour Leaders working for Elzenhof, a Flemish cultural centre located in Brussels, refused to include the African Museum as part of their 'Matongé wandelingen' ('Matongé walks'). These are guided visits to the borough of Matongé, the African neighborhood of Brussels. Initially, it was of particular interest to people living outside Brussels. Overtime, it has become more and more touristy and has even been taken up by other organizations. I had once been part as an apprentice on their team and, as such, I was allowed to accompany a Tour Leader a couple of times during guided visits through the Matongé borough. My aim was to add this experience on an application form for work as a Tour Leader abroad. As the only black Tour Leader, they were quite happy to have me on their team. I guess they hoped that way to lessen tensions a bit. Even tough Tour Leaders try to be as less voyeuristic as possible so as not to hurt the feelings of the inhabitants, there have been a lot of complaints from people living there who felt that they were being look at as monkeys living in cages. Well, in truth their complaints were not entirely unjustified. During these visits, people get to discover a little bit more about the history of Matongé, the first wave of Congolese migrants who came to settle there and how it has since fit in with other neighbourhoods. Tourists receive also a few tips about good African restaurants and where to find some specific African products. Tour leaders are allowed to plan their visits the way the feel by adding a few things of their own they find interesting to talk about. During a meeting, I had suggested to also include a visit to the African Museum. None of the tour leaders seemed much enthusiastic to do so. One young woman tour Leader during the meeting said: 'these people are really stuck in time there.' Anyway, why was I not entitled to a bit of positive discrimination? I cannot think of anything more surreal.

Enjoy poverty

The greatest hypocrites of all are unquestionably to be found in the NGO sector but who would have ever thought that? In the nineties, the first time I went for an interview for anything related to this sector was for an NGO organization called *Werkgroep Integratie Vluchtelingen* in Mechelen. It deals with all kinds of issues regarding political refugees, by offering them structures and advice on how best to integrate society. At that time, it was still in its infancy and a very small NGO; nothing to do with what it has become down the years. They were looking for an administrative assistant. The candidates, as they wrote in their job ad, did not need to have any kind of degree but dedication and the ability to identify himself with most of the problems political refugees are faced with. I explained in my cover letter that some members of my own family were confronted with exactly the same problems mentioned in the job ad. This was not surprising: every African family knows someone who is either a political refugee or has problems with his stay in Belgium. Logically, they must have been aware of this too. So I got invited for a job interview.

The panel consisted of four people, one of whom was a nun. In the course of the interview, out of the blue, one of them asked me whether I had seen this documentary called *Makak* on the VRT, a Flemish channel. It was a documentary, filmed with a hidden camera by two young Moroccans, about the way they were discriminated against on a daily basis. As it happened, I had seen it and had been quite shocked by it. This documentary had caused some shock waves throughout Flanders and had made many people feel uncomfortable; so Flemings tried to play it down as best as they could. Well, they may have had some compelling reasons to do so. By that time, Arabs already had lost their status as victims, and this was not entirely unjustified. Besides, I do not think that the VRT, which likes to pass itself off as such a forward-thinking channel, would ever dare to show it again without incurring ridicule after everything people have seen with Moroccans. But then again, you never know with this channel. Immune to ridicule, they even have an anti-discrimination chart on their website while they are practically not people from foreign background working for their channel. Anyway, were the problems of Moroccans in any way more important than mine? I asked myself. I never gave a shit about the problems they are confronted with, nor did I expect them to care about mine. Then, this stupid nun was asked me, taking care of slowly enunciating every word as correctly as she could as if she was speaking to Friday from Robinson Crusoë, if I was used to meeting people from foreign backgrounds. I told her as kindly as I could that, as a black person, it seemed logical I did. It made the rest of them laugh, trying to distract the attention from her ridiculous question.

Then came a moment, I started to talk spontaneously about the plight of Bruno, telling them how as a construction engineer, he had already sent more than a hundred CVs without getting even a single appointment for an interview, but that did not seem to interest them. They probably didn't even believe what I told them. To make that clear, two of the women started to speak aloud about some shopping they still had to do. I felt humiliated, but it was only afterwards that the whole thing started to sink in. They no longer considered me as a real foreigner because they thought my Flemish sounded too good to be that of a foreigner.

The first time I read in a job profile that candidates should have a deep understanding of the 'North-South' relations was from a job ad of Oxfam. This kind of crap is mentioned in practically every job ad description related to the NGO sector. The fact that some people who apply could actually be a product of this 'North-South' relationship and embody both sides, seem never to have crossed their minds. Other typical Flemish job ads for example are ads like 'would you like to come to work in a multicultural environment?' Like one that appeared on the website of an organisation called Prisma based in Mechelen. Basically what they meant was whether you are up to come to work in an environment among some Moroccans and maybe a few blacks around. A job ad published by a NGO called Pag-Asa, a Flemish organisation that combats human trafficking, described a successful applicant as one 'that likes to work with foreigners' and 'perceives diversity as a challenge.' In fact, in their case like in most other cases, what they meant was that the people you were going to come into contact with were most likely to be from foreign backgrounds, but not concerning their workforce which is entirely white. I should know; I once went there for a job interview. Still in 2010, the Flemish website of the Red Cross described successful candidates in their job ads, as requiring things like 'feeling comfortable working with foreigners.' Extract of a job ad on the website of the Red Cross for someone to guide refugees and for which you need <u>experience</u> working with foreigners:

Over Rode Kruis (The Red Cross)

<u>Print</u>

Medisch begeleider Opvangcentrum voor asielzoekers, Sint-Niklaas

Rode Kruis-Vlaanderen biedt asielzoekers een tijdelijke thuis. Een dynamisch team houdt het opvangcentrum draaiend. Onderdak, maaltijden, begeleiding en veiligheid vormen de spil van de werking.

Je oriënteert mensen in hun nieuwe verblijfplaats en zorgt voor ondersteuning in de lopende procedures. Daarnaast staat het welzijn van de asielzoekers en families centraal. Je speelt in op de noden van bewoners en zorgt zo voor een rustpunt.

Jouw profiel:
- Je beschikt over een diploma verpleegkunde
- Je hebt ervaring in werken met allochtonen
- Je beschikt over een goede mondelinge taalvaardigheid (N,F,E,D)
- Je bent een organisatietalent en administratief nauwkeurig
- Je beschikt over goede communicatieve vaardigheden en bent flexibel

- Je bent bereid in een ploegenstelsel te werken met weekendprestaties

Plaats van tewerkstelling:
Rode Kruis-Vlaanderen, Opvangcentrum Sint-Niklaas, Kasteelstraat 8, 9100 Sint-Niklaas

Interesse?
Solliciteer online (gelieve je CV en motivatiebrief toe te voegen).

Bijkomende info : Departement Opvang Asielzoekers, Pascale Vandekerckhove, 015/ 44 35 49

"Je hebt ervaring in werken met allochtonen" means literally "you do have experience working with foreigners". These type of job ads descriptions coming from francophone run social organisations or francophone NGOS are just unthinkable. This was still only the beginning of what I was to discover about the NGO sector, not to mention their condescending, patronising manners unlike anything I had ever experienced until then. One such event that springs to mind was at a Christian inspired NGO for combating blindness in Africa called "Light for the World" located in Brussels. The vacancy had been posted on a Flemish website. Yet from the moment Geert Vanneste who was the head of the program and going to interview opened the door to welcome me, he immediately started to speak French to me with a thick Flemish accent. During the entire interview, he always came back to the fact that I spoke so well Flemish. In fact, as so many people are, he was intrigued by my fluency and wanted to know how this had come about. It tired me and trying to contain my irritation, I asked him whether this was actually an advantage or not?

"An advantage of course!" he said.

"So why then," I asked, "do you keep coming back to this?" He started to blush and felt embarrassed. I could see that he wanted to end the interview. Next day, I sent him a message telling him that he and his colleague were stuck in time and that he should not consider my candidacy any further. Despite all this, it amazed me that during our conversation he acknowledged, without feigning surprise upon my raising the subject, that they were indeed so few blacks in the NGO sector in Belgium. The NGO sector in Belgium is unsurprisingly entirely run by white people. I can testify to that. I went practically to all of them for a job interview: Oxfam, Max Havelaar and their fair-trade bullshit, 11.11.11, you name it. A Congolese doctor friend of mine, Doctor Didier N'Gay, told me they never really expected us to apply there.

The only blacks I see coming from this sector are the ones they put on posters during their campaigns for donations or these charity muggers roaming the streets harassing people by trying to sell things on behalf of their respective NGOs. I guess their bosses must be telling them:

"We do so much for you guys! Is that not the least you can do for us in return? Get out there!"

I cannot think of anything more hateful and disgusting than the NGO sector. The truth is that most of these NGOs or social organizations still barely bother to answer your applications. Another thing that struck me wherever I went to present myself for a job interview, was that when there were any people from foreign backgrounds around, they were mostly women as if they feel threatened by men from foreign backgrounds. The Belgians would be prepared to help the whole world as long as it would create them job opportunities that they could then share among themselves. It is not about trying to 'change the world for the better' which is a massive deception, but most of all their own. Put it simply: it is just a question of jobs.

From time to time Bruno would see these lads working for various Belgian NGOs in Congo, happy not to have any dealings with them. As he once said:

"They're all guys with Flemish outlooks:" The Helmut Lotti type of guys. They are perceived by the Congolese as a new type of mercenaries. By the time I came to visit Bruno - he had already been there for more than six years - he never met one Belgian-Congolese working as an expatriate for a NGO from Belgium. Locals, yes; but

Belgian-Congolese who would enjoy the same luxuries like these new mercenaries by living in comfortable homes, earning obscene amounts of money and driving around in SUVs, nope. For a good insight into the inner murky world of all these NGOs, I can only suggest the documentary of Renzo Martens - 'Enjoy Poverty.' It is probably one of the most disturbing documentaries I have ever seen. After seeing this, I think anyone should better understand why white people are so keen to come to work in developing countries. Yet, somehow, these NGOs seem so convinced of their moral authority that they do not hesitate to gleefully criticize someone like the controversial Belgian-Congolese businessman George Forrest. He is the boss of Malta Forrest, still one of the biggest construction companies in Congo, and had often been criticized for being corrupt and because of his dubious links with the powers that be; as if any NGO was able to get things done there in such a corrupt country without any links at all. He had even been accused for being the linchpin regarding the looting of the country's mineral resources. His harshest critics always stem from the Flemish corner, as if he was supposed to be a saint. On a Flemish channel, he said that they should better start controlling all these people from the NGOs driving around in their SUV's.

"Doing precisely what?" he added. This white man has done more for my country by offering people jobs, constructing hospitals, schools and other vital necessities than all the NGOs put together. The same could be said for Sylvèstre Bwira Kyahi who, despite all the good work he does for the people there, does not get recognised by the international NGOs for the simple fact that he did not want to let them take over control of his local NGOs. This man is just terrific and deserves all the praise and western media attention he can get not because, for a change, he would be gay and wants to marry his lover - the kind of stories the western media are so fond of - but just for all his good deeds. Normally, it is always white people who get all the accolades, lots of press when they are helping out the most needy. They get books written about them and movie deals. I am sure that most black people are familiar with these movie posters about yet another white man/woman surrounded mother Theresa-like by only blacks, having done something wonderful to get those poor little Negroes ahead in life or having fought for their rights. What would the black man be without the white man, isn't it? Aren't we the white man's burden? Well, for a change, it would be nice to see a movie made about Sylvèstre Bwira, with him in the middle on a movie poster this time, surrounded by all these white vultures from their respective NGOs. He is, together with Patrice Lumumba, one of the greatest personalities Congo has ever known.

I wished that President Joseph Kabila would impose a quota of Belgian-Congolese people concerning all these NGOs from Belgium coming to work there.

One woman I knew called Erica who had worked in this sector said that catholic inspired NGOs were probably the worse. She had worked for the NGO World Villages. She told me how some people she worked with almost fainted at the mere mention of words like 'contraceptives' or 'condoms' as if there was nothing more immoral; and how every week she received letters of complaints from people tired of being harassed for even more money, after they had agreed to adopt a child by donating a certain amount of money every month so that it could go to school and for other vital stuff. These letters came by the dozens. She was asked to ignore them. Most of their personnel working abroad had been involved time and again in matters of child abuse. Yet they seemed somehow to live in self-denial about it telling her once that those acts were actually not committed by paedophiles but by gay men.

The one event to top it all in the NGO sector and just could not get any more surreal was when I went to present myself for a job interview in 2009 at Ucos (www.ucos.be) a Flemish organisation in Brussels that tries to bring students from Flemish universities in contact with Congolese students in my country. I had never heard of such an organisation before. They were looking for a tour Leader to accompany students once a year to Lubumbashi, in Congo. Anyone would think this would be something for me, with my outgoing personality and globetrotter experience. I was interviewed by three

103

white people. One was the president of this organisation who, quite frankly, said she had never been in Congo; the other one was a young lady who seemed to have no travel experience at all, which was understandable for she was still too young; the last one, a guy, had been there two times. They were Flemish people through and through, the kind I have never felt comfortable with. For a Congolese to be included in the interviewing panel would have been a too revolutionary idea for these people. Actually, I do not think it would have been that simple for them to find one either. I sensed that they did not have any real black friends or acquaintances in their private lives. I also could sense from what they were saying or by the content of their questions that they did not have any links at all with Brussels, but came most likely from Flemish peasant towns. Actually, I even wonder whether they really intended to invite me for an interview because I had to remind them of my application as happened so many times.

The president of the organisation, a fat cow, asked me:

"Why do you think you would be the ideal candidate for the job?" (What an original question!) I answered with what seemed the most obvious reply:

"Because I know how we are," I said laconically. I had also been asked to make suggestions from a program they showed me about the way they intended to run things during a trip to Lubumbashi for which, among other things, they had planned debates on colonialism from books written only, of course, by white authors and other kinds of activities. I wondered if these people had ever heard of African writers, let alone black writers. The whole thing I read from their program oozed Flemish thinking and idealism with words like 'sustainable tourism' and 'gender.' I tried to explain to them that the word 'tourism' still sounded strange to most Congolese people there and to be cautious with the word 'gender.' Anyone is allowed to say a lot to Congolese women but, oh dear, do not dare to criticise their men. As gentle as I could, I tried to explain to these Flemish peasants that people are getting tired being told what to do, tired of their (white) universalism and their way of looking at things. Anyway, they did not hire me. This guy told me on the telephone that they had been more looking for someone with an educational background - strange, there was no mention of that in the job ad - but nevertheless asked me if I would be interested to participate in workshops to underline the 'cultural exchange.' I declined the offer. I do not think that this lad ever realised his contradictions and how insulting he was. He made me think of those bygone eras when zoos used people of colour as accessories to exhibit or the expo 58 - the world expo hosted in Brussels in 1958- where at the *'Pavillon Congolais,'* they had set up a whole little African village with real Africans who were supposed to enact life in my country and were thrown bananas by the crowd. Some Africans were so appalled by their treatment that they left the exposition the same day. It could be of course that nowadays they would have tried to show more understanding for such things by postings signs near my workshop, saying 'FEEDING OR THROWING BANANAS ARE STRICTLY FORBIDDEN.' For some reason it even made me think of myself as some kind of modern version of Sara Baartman when she was exhibited as a freak attraction in the nineteenth century under the name 'Hottentot Venus' and had to entertain people by showing her unusual large buttocks. I wonder how they would have presented me during their 'cultural exchange,' as the 'Hottentot of Brussels'? The truth is that I do not think that many people, and I am especially alluding to the women, would have been that enthralled by the sight of my arse though: I haven't got any, and I certainly would not have gone about sending the wrong signals only to end up with unwanted attention. This young lady had been asking me a few questions about this 'cultural exchange' thing and I never knew exactly what to say. I tried to explain to her that in Brussels that is no big issue. Told her that the day before, I had been to an open-air swimming pool in Ottignies with a bunch of friends, amongst whom was a Moroccan lad, an Italian and two polish girls and that, as far as I could remember, this did not lead to any passionate conversation about 'cultural exchange.' I had completely forgotten that for some sad people, in order to make a statement, to shore up one's progressive credentials it is still a big thing to be seen with an Arab, a black or any anyone with a foreign background for that matter; but preferably still, someone from a minority group with a more 'controversial' reputation. That having just normal relations which include tensions, fights as well as nice moments, the normal things any relations are based on seems unthinkable for some people; and that for these sad people everything had always to be put in a context of open-mindedness, 'cultural exchange,' and idealism. What are such depressing people doing in my country? Who the fuck likes Flemings anyway? Not that I was looking forward to be on the go with Flemish students but it would have been better than any desk-bound job.

Chapter 7

Allah is great!
He ain't for me

Being discriminated against can sometimes be a godsend. If during a certain period of my life I had found work for even a short time, I would never have been entitled to a social flat when a fire broke out on my floor. How this how this came about does not really matter. Shit happens everywhere. I was entitled to social benefits and as such was what in Belgium is called a social case *pure sang*. Instead of pursuing these vain goals trying to make something out of myself, they probably wanted me to be this way from the beginning. The only time I found work during that period was for a short period of time in an insurance company and at another company called Reprobel, in both, as an administrative assistant. At the latter, I was supposed to be taken on indefinitely after this girl whom I had come to replace decided to come back. I had been in a state of total shock when the firemen woke me up early one morning to rescue me, as one could imagine, and quite affected through it all. It had broken out in the attic, then spread to the roof leaving big holes in it that could be seen from outside. The ceiling of my kitchen had broken down at some places, but it was above all my neighbour's apartment that sustained most damage. For security reasons, we were not allowed to live there any longer. At the police station, a female cop tried to reassure me.

"Everything is going to be all right," she said. Since I had no place left to go, I was entitled to stay one week in a hotel for free, breakfasts included for the time being until they found a 'solution.' I was so move by their gentleness that I could barely hold back my tears and almost started to take at face value what they keep telling us: The police are your friend! Anyway, it is always nice to know but I had even more pressing matters at hand, which of course, they knew nothing about: I had an appointment at four o'clock in Leuven with a guy I met on Taxistop (hitchhiking service) to go to Prague with. I was hoping this was going to take my mind off things after such an ordeal. Poor me! A close friend told me that, now that I was basically homeless due to a fire, these were terrific points to put on application form to be entitled to a social flat. The procedures got speeded up thanks to someone my friend knew at the housing association called 'Foyer Anderlechtois.' Getting out of this area started to be an obsession. I had always hated living there but even in my wildest dreams I never thought that this was going to be possible thanks to a fire. Apparently, some fires can be life-changing. Bruno and one of his best mates had bought this apartment blocks on the 'Rue van Lint' nearby the City Hall of Anderlecht. It is one of the most deprived, run-down, areas one can think of and a foretaste of what Brussels is heading to: its rampant islamization. Now for some reason from the moment a white person says that, he is immediately branded a racist and supposed to have links with right extremist groups. So I wonder where that puts me in as a black person saying this. Do I also fit the profile? The truth is that it bewilders just about everyone; whites as well as people from foreign backgrounds who are not Muslims.

I never got used to neighbourhoods with veiled women and their lovely smiling faces, mosques on every corner of the street, satellite dishes on every house and everything else that characterizes such neighbourhoods. Most people who live there feel ashamed and trapped for being unable to find an apartment to rent for a decent price elsewhere. Ironically, even some Arabs I spoke with felt this way; maybe because they felt that the non-Muslims still left were waiting too long to embrace Islam. I sometimes wonder whether Arabs are aware of this entire mass movement taking place on their behalf and if they know that people used to describe the quality of a neighbourhood by its slight level of 'arabization' or not. That even foreigners, me included, would say during the summer when it is nice weather things like "let's go to an open air swimming pool, its Ramadan it won't be full with Arabs yet." So it is not necessarily real

Belgians who speak like that but just about everyone. Are all these people racist?

I got a nice apartment with a communal garden and a little lawn in front. The apartment blocks were only three stories high and were surrounded by a park. It was an idyllic place, I could not ask for more. After years of living in the area I came from, I had forgotten that they were still places like that. I was scared to death of ending up in one of those places affected by gangs and drugs. My new place was evenly cosmopolitan without feeling invaded by one particular kind of people or culture, neither of which particularly appealed to me. This may sound a bit ironic because the lad, a close friend of mine who made it all possible, happened to be a Moroccan. So what?

Years later, when we received a notice from the housing association that they were going to rehouse us because of repairs, we were all scared to death about where we were going to end up. It is needless to say that what petrified us most was the thought of ending up in any kind of couscous neighbourhood. From the moment I met a tenant it was the main discussion point of the day. Knowing that they were going to rehouse us in the same town (Anderlecht) and with not that many nice places - maybe the word 'civilised' would be more appropriate - with social apartments around, our greatest fear was to be rehoused to these huge apartment blocks on the 'Rue des Goujons.' This place is like the end of the world, the favelas of Brussels. It is basically an Arab city on its own. Ending up there is like having been stripped of your dignity. One day, riding past these apartment blocks on my bike, I saw a Belgian flag hanging high above someone's balcony as if he was sending out a SOS trying to remind everyone that there was still a Belgian left. I was again among the lucky ones! I ended up in a pleasant neighbourhood, and it was my best friend ever, Abdel, that help me to move all my stuff with a van that a friend had lent him. The truth is that I had gone on my own initiative to the housing association, asking if I could speak with a social assistant there. From the moment I detected in his accent that he was Flemish, I immediately started to speak to him in Flemish. It worked miracles! I had quite frankly told him that I did not want to end up again in any kind couscous neighbourhood and been approached every day by young Moroccans who inspire such intense disgust to just about everyone. They could be so original! They would usually start with things like: "*Hé mon frère!*" (Hey bruv!) If I dared to ignore them, they would rather say: "*Hé azé!*" (Moroccan word for black!) Or "*nègro*" (nigger) or, in the worst case, "*zemmel*" (Moroccan word for faggot).

Considering everything I know about them, having a Moroccan judging someone because he might be gay is, for me, still one of the greatest jokes I can think of. Because of my dreadlocks, I knew damn well what they are after: trying to sell me some dope. Another close Moroccan friend of mine had been searching for an apartment for more than a year until he found a decent neighbourhood where his son would not grow up with only people from his own race, as they usually do, but rather interact with all kinds of people. In my neighbourhood, there was a Call shop owned by Syrian Christians. I used to go there almost every day. One day, the mother of the guy who owned the Call shop told me that her son had bought a nice apartment in Ever.

"It is a really nice there," she said, and after first looking around for fear that someone might overhear what she was about to say, she added in her broken French:

"*Il n'y a pas encore beaucoup d'Arabes,*" (There are not many Arabs yet). By then, she had been in Belgium for only then years. Yet she enjoyed chatting with Moroccan women customers. It sounded a bit ironic to me because a few days earlier, I met a nephew of my black family who told me that my niece, his sister, had found a nice apartment situated in Woluwé St Pierre and had said exactly the same thing. I remember that it started to make me dream and wonder "could there still be a few towns in Brussels that have not been invaded yet by Arabs and their Islam?"

I can perfectly understand that most Muslims would rather be in a neighbourhood they can identify with. I can even understand that some of them would not mind to have a muezzin on top of a mosque to call on the faithful for prayer, or at least have its wailing tape recorded so that it can be heard all around the neighbourhood like it is already the case in some places in Holland. Personally, as a kaffir, I would rather have none of that and I am sure that most Muslims would perfectly understand that. After all, is this religion not about peace and understanding? This is not cheap Islam bashing; it is just that where my street is concerned, I do not want this feeling of living in any kind of Islamic society but preferably in a laic one, which is my right anyway. On top of that, I am sure that this must rather please Muslim women, too, logically. Don't they want men to feel attracted to them? Well, what can I say other than mission accomplished! Having said that, one cannot help but laugh seeing how some of these women would wear their nikaq, hijab, burka, kebab or whatever it is they put on their heads as a political statement or emblem against western culture and its values - which is of course their right - yet find themselves just westernised enough to be entitled to any social benefits at hand. I even witnessed some of these women starting spontaneously to sing 'La Brabançonne' (the national anthem) on their way to cash their welfare checks.

For no reason at all every black person in this country has been at least once racially abused by Moroccans acting as if they were real Belgians. Concerning me, the most striking event was the day I went with friends from my town to the 'Lokerse feesten' which is a music festival that last ten days. I went there to see the reggae group Doctor Alimentado. Over the years, this event got so big that they even managed to bill Jamiroquai or Burning Spear (my favourite reggae group) as top act. I had seen from afar how a group of youths got more and more excited when they noticed me. Once I drew level with them, I instantly felt that this was too great a challenge for them to let go - well, certainly in those days anyway - and how they were struggling with themselves before it all erupted, as I had expected, and subjected me to all kind of racist abuse. But, perhaps, what was most shocking was to notice among the group a Moroccan lad. I remember thinking to have seen it all. It is difficult to explain to anyone what goes through your head in such moments, being insulted by someone from the most hated minority group in Belgium acting as if he was a real Belgian. Being racially taunted by couscous people was not new of course, but it was the first time it happened to me in the company of real Belgians.

At the Vaartkapoen, a Flemish cultural centre in Molenbeek, an ex-work colleague, a Congolese woman had lived in the Arab enclave of Molenbeek. A town, as Bruno Reynders (minister of foreign affairs) described was no longer part of Belgium anymore. She told me how every day she got bullied, racially abused, spat at and even got her car set on fire just because she dared to stand up to these young Moroccans thugs for whatever reason. This woman had been through a living hell in this neighbourhood and her story was quite well known at the Vaartkapeon. I have often been wondering whether their hate was as much motivated by her physical appearance. She was a very tall and quite imposing woman, radiating kindness and intelligence but what was most striking was the darkness of her skin which is quite rare among Congolese women; I thought she was from Senegal. This must have been too confusing for these young Moroccans thugs. How could this woman look like that and at the same time be so articulate? Had this been a story - this is something everyone knows in Belgium - about a Moroccan family that would have been through the same ordeal, there would have been such an outcry and been talked about on every kind of media outlet one can think of. Philipe Moureaux, the Mayor of Molenbeek, would have made sure to keep this story alive for as long as it could in the media and on Maghreb TV. He is the new Saladin and great defender of the Muslim population in Molenbeek; the Muslims love him, too. They love each other so much that the Mayor could not resist at the age of 75 to marry a Moroccan woman 40 years younger than him. No one is allowed to say anything too critical about the Moroccan community of his town or he gets ballistic. When some journalists denounced the fact that some Muslims MP's from his political party, *Le Partie Socialiste*, did not even bother to translate their pamphlets send in Turkish or Arab into French or Dutch to their constituency during election time, he started to speak about racism and comparing those journalists with Joseph Goebbels.

Racism for *le Partie Socialiste* and Ecolo - one of the worst political parties in history - has been reduced on whether or not you love an Arab-Muslim and on how far you are prepare to tolerate this rampant islamization all around you. The rest does not count for these people which could partly explain why racism stemming from Moroccans is still a taboo subject for some people, as if they were the ultimate victims when it comes down to racism. Media wise, I do not think that anyone would make many headlines in Belgium by saying something denigrating or critical - justified or not - about let say the Congolese, Brazilian or Polish community, but do not try to say something bad about Moroccans. On the contrary, things have gotten so pathetic that when something bad happens to someone from this community, everyone is forced out of bed at night with the implicit message to show some concern. Another thing that's also quite striking is that only a white person is always supposed to be racist. For some reason a white person committing a racist act will always be more mediatise than the other way around; as if racism against whites did not count.

During a job interview at the Vaartkapeon, I was asked whether it did not disturb me to come to work every day in the Arab enclave of Molenbeek. When I told this to some of my Moroccans friends, they did not believe me at first. During Ramadan, a Moroccan woman had been passing around some biscuits she had prepared. I told my direct boss who had also been present during my interview, that I did not like these Moroccan biscuits neither their food in general. Trying to laugh, she asked me whether I was not being a bit of a racist.

I sometimes wonder whether all these white people, in their aseptic world of political correctness, couscous meals or Arabic poetry evenings ever had any real friends among the migrant community or people from foreign backgrounds at all. I mean friends that come over to sleep at your place sometimes, go on holiday with, row and make friends with again. People we call real friends. I do not think that these people are even slightly aware of the contempt directed towards them from us, foreigners, or of the way we laugh at them behind their backs. The most disgusting racist remarks I had to endure throughout my life came from these very kinds of people, the so-called anti-racist ones. They are the ones I hate the most. I do not care about their level of culture, IQ or whatever degrees they possess. These people never had to go through anything I went through. Besides, if I ever told them they probably would not want to hear me out; it might be just too much to digest for them. My hate and disdain is so great towards them that, if only I had an opportunity, I would defecate in front of them without having to think twice about it. However, somehow I do not think that this would upset them that much either for in their delirium of open-mindedness, they probably would try to rationalize the whole incident by asking their friends not to take offence at it. It must not be difficult to imagine one of such conversations playing out like this around of cup of tea:

"For *these people* it is just another way to express themselves, you know?" one of them would say.

"Just look at Chris Ofili, the Ghanaian artist; did he not play with shit too when he made his famous Holy Virgin Mary entirely made up of elephant dung?" Another one would remind them.

"Oh yeah I remember that! Another person would say. I wonder how he got access to that pile of elephant dung, probably from a zoo or something". And with knowing glances at each other, one would conclusively say:

"You see, it is just an integral part of the way they are. These people enjoy playing with shit."

In this backward town where I grew up, a young Moroccan kid once shouted at me, "Hey bamboula!" while I was waiting at a bus stop; just like that. He was from a Moroccan family that had come to live there in the nineties and lived two blocks from my house. His father was quite a character. Except for his western dress, he was the stereotypical Arab. Whenever he walked down the street, his woman would be ahead of him with their kids whilst he would be following at a certain distance behind. Still, I do not think he would have allowed her to take the kids with her, should she ever had to walk through a minefield. His house was just in front of the pub of my godfather who, in his opinion, did not respect the law on noise. This argument would have come as a surprise or even as a joke to anyone in such a sleepy town where everything already starts to close down in the late afternoon. This would be an ideal place for someone like Spencer Tunick if he would not be too bothered by onlookers to make his nude pictures while his people, who otherwise would have been arrested for exhibitionisms, are now allowed to undress themselves and go about naked in the name of art. It is amazing to what lengths white people are prepare to go as long as it is in the name of art or even for medical reasons like in the TV series "embarrassing bodies" in which deranged exhibitionists flaunt their complaints by showing their most intimate parts to a doctor in the presence of a camera.

Anyway, it is only during the summer that things start to wake up a bit, but I am not sure that an outsider would easily notice the change. With more youths around, some even coming from out of town, there would a bit more noise than usual in this pub as might be expect; just the natural chain of events. It also happened, although rarely, that on any Saturday nights, things might have been a bit more rowdy than usual, just like everywhere else. Not that I was there much to witness it, but sooner or later, I would come to know it. In a town where nothing ever happens, people would never have passed such an opportunity to make a big deal out of it. My mother too would certainly have joined the chorus.

Well, for this Arab, all of that had to change from now on. So the day after, he stood at the front of his door and started yelling at anyone coming out of the pub about what happened the night before and inevitably this ended up in a slanging match. As happens so often in such cases, one day it climaxed. One early evening, he stood outside his door because of the noise again and then started to shout at a group of youths who had gathered outside the pub. At first, like me, they did not even seem to know what he was so mad about. He just kept shouting on and on; he even cited aloud some paragraphs from the textbook on noise. Later that night, he started all over again and then rang at everyone's door in the neighbourhood as if he was trying to drum up some support for his cause. He just looked out of himself, convinced to have Allah on his side. I will never forget how at one point he went up the driveway to ring at the door of our former house doctor. This man came to open the door in his pyjamas and just nodded at him. He was an old man and was starting to suffer from senility. Anyone who has already witnessed a few things about Arabs, would still have been taken aback, even shocked. The innate barbarity of these people seems like a second nature to them. In a short space of time, this Arab had become a celebrity in his own right but somehow also a barrel of laugh, really. When Bruno needed to go to the police station for a certain document, a cop asked him how our famous neighbour was doing. Then they all started to laugh their heads off.

This Arab also accused me once of harassing his wife. Whenever I went shopping, I would meet his wife too. I remember finding this a bit embarrassing but I would always greet her politely. I wonder what might have gone through her mind saying "hello" to such barbaric people. Yet, I never could imagine that such an ugly woman would have seen anything more to it when her husband came to ring at my door one day. I happened not to be there, it was Bruno who opened the door.

"I heard your brother has been harassing my wife again," he said straightaway not even giving time to my brother to say something. "I warn you both, this is the last time and I hope I made myself clear on this" he said wagging his finger as a last warning before leaving. Despite all this, I did envy him. He did not give a shit about being appreciated or not. This very idea must have looked completely idiotic to him. If anything, as it is the case of many people of his community in Belgium, he seemed to thrive on disgust. The way he walked around the streets was as if he owned the place. I really do admire how Arabs managed to impose their will on society under the guise of tolerance. A tolerance that is not always visible from their side in some boroughs in Brussels or Antwerp. It is a well-known fact that in some boroughs with a high Muslims population, people have implicitly to follow their rules. Shop owners dare not sell alcohol or pork out of fear to see their businesses vandalized or burned down;

girls, who are not necessarily Muslims, wear veils in order to be respected and not to be treated as sluts. In the name of maintaining a good social cohesion between all the different communities from foreign backgrounds, these kinds of allegations are always swept under the rug. People who insist too much on speaking publicly about it are immediately branded as racists and supposed to have links with right-wings groups. Well, I will say it once again: except for the palm of my hands and feet, I am black! And as far as I know I am not a member of any right-extremist group or a racist. Even if I was, I must be a racist of a rare breed. All my mates are foreigners just like me and my closest friends are Moroccans. Growing older I don't like to be that much with Belgians anymore whether he is a Fleming or Walloon doesn't matter.

Things we thought would never happen here, like in Trappes where some fanatics managed to impose their rule on an entire estate in France, are becoming reality in some neighbourhoods in Brussels. For some Muslims, even the simple fact to see kaffirs enjoying themselves seems to disturb them. I once went to a big party organized by the nightclub in Brussels called 'The fuse' at the coast in Ostend. During the summer, Ostend is one of the nicest cities in the world. It was one of those days that made me aware how nice a place Belgium could be if only there would be a little more sun. I worked as an employee for an insurance company, earn good money and just felt good about myself. It was during the week and I had left sooner from work that day to meet up with friends at the coast. I played football on the beach and later on went to visit family friends in Middelkerke. At the party you could hear the best techno, house music there is, everyone seemed like in a trance. The atmosphere was so great, so positive that no-one could ever have imagined that this would come to be spoiled by fights that night. During the evening, I had seen two Arabs. I could easily notice them, or they me for that matter, for they were very few foreigners around. Yet it would be these two Arabs - I do not think that for many people in Belgium this would come as a surprise - that later got involved in that fight. Not that they had much time to do anything as the bouncers were quick to react. What I did not understand was that one of them still found it worthwhile to come back after everything seemed to have settled down. He stayed outside pointing at his pocket and pretending he was carrying a gun; a message intended for the lad who stood next to me inside. Anyone can behave like a fool sometimes, but a normal person would have felt a bit embarrassed about what had just happened and leave, trying to forget things as quickly as possible. Not so for Arabs. On the contrary, time and time again they seem hell-bent on causing trouble everywhere they show up. I wonder whether at some point, Arabs feel the need to clear up this mess by seeing all this alcohol flowing around and other kaffir-like things; as if they had to put an end to all this 'moral decay' like someone who just had received a 'calling' from heaven. Or maybe it is just their way to get back at kaffirs by spoiling everyone else's happiness. They know damn well they have got nothing nice about themselves. They are, together with Chinese people, the least attractive people I can think of. No one really likes their presence at whatever it is. I am not just talking about the Belgians - I do not care about them - but just about everyone. Wherever Moroccans show up, there are always tensions. Maybe they should make a sequel on this controversial documentary called 'Makak.'

Chapter 8

London Calling

Just after the turn of the century, I went to London to stay for the first time at my younger brother Max's apartment. He lived nearby the King's Cross station in a council block on the 'Caledonian road.' I had already travelled everywhere but I had never been to London, which was an irony that was not lost on some of the punters I talked to in a pub. It was beautiful weather and I suggested organising a day's trip to Brighton. Max was all excited at the prospect because he had never been there nor had he ever been to Blackpool; one of the most popular tourist destinations for Brits. Just like for so many Congolese in Belgium the only places he seemed to know were those where Congolese people met. He never acquired a British accent either but spoke rather with a lovely Nigerian accent. The type of accent that always gave me the feeling of being constantly brutalized when spoken to, and yet he was born there. Truth be told, he also spent a great deal of his youth in Angola but most of his life he spent in England. Another thing that quite struck me is that he did not seem to have the slightest contact with whites, let alone black Britons, except at work I guess. It had always been painful for me to find a conversation that might interest both of us; and to think that I almost definitely left Belgium to stay at his place. While walking around Brixton, a black woman was surprised at the way we jumped from French to English when we spoke to each other, and started to chat with us. She told us that she worked for the railway network and that they were desperate for multilingual people and then asked me if I would not be interested in applying there. Of course, I was interested! I had always looked up to Britain. It is my culture in a way. I am more hooked on British channels than French ones. I have become quite alienated from French culture. Even though I still find England one of the most depressing countries paradoxically there are so many things I like about Britain. To start with their worldly known sense of humour for example and the fact that they have a much better sense of race relations unlike in Belgium. Yes, I know that a black man in Britain is seven times more likely to be stop and search than a white person. But then again, Brussels does not have this knife problem which is a typical black thing, and this gang culture of young black teenagers wanting to play out their fantasies of gang warfare like in the USA. Britain is certainly not a nice place when a person is born on the wrong end of the stick as the 'August riots' has shown. It is the country with the least social mobility of all the industrious nations. Despite knowing a lot about London, there are some places in London I did not know were such pockets of misery and rather a reminder of a Charles dickens era. Some cities in Belgium like Charleroi or La Louvière, which are economically considered as '*région sinistre*' (devastated region) are sunny places compared to some inner-city areas in England.

Yet, despite all this, I could not wait to go. The only thing that made me a bit wary was Max's apartment. It was a bit cramped and I had to sleep in the living room, but that was not my main worry. It was the fact that he had few friends and that I did not want to be too much the centre of his attention. For someone who likes to be on his own from time to time, this would have been too much for me to bear. I was also a bit wary on how the evenings were going to be. His wife could spend the whole evening watching all kinds of music channels and probably complain whenever he was not around, on how she felt 'deceived' by him.

My younger brother is rather a real African and not really the most refined man I have ever met; his manner could be quite rough sometimes. Despite having been highly educated and having a good paid job in the pharmaceutical industry, he has this kind of typical man-eating African fierceness about him that makes me understand why some white people might think we still have fondness for human flesh. Or to put it more mildly, I do not think that anyone would ever caught him singing love songs to his wife whilst playing the harp or singing '*solo mio*' with tears in his eyes while having both hands on his

120

chest. Besides, I do not even know whether he knows that song. Even people who are not used to blacks in general would never take him for a black Briton. I cannot imagine that his desperate attempt in trying to pass off as a real Briton by saying "*innit*" for just about anything did ever fool anyone. This refine couple met each other in Congo, so it would be grotesque to think that she ever expected soap inspired ('I love you *pour toujours*,' 'I miss you,' 'Comeback') tenderness from him. There is not much of that depressing bullshit, soapy complications, to start a relation out there. Things may indeed be a more rough, or less subtle, but so what? In the end, the whole thing boils down to money anyway, just like in every other part of the world. On the other hand, his wife had never set foot in Europe before they decided to marry, but she seemed to have done some catching up where drama is concerned by watching 'The Eastenders' or any of those imbecilic girly soaps. One evening while I was alone with her, this lump of fat tried to play 'the one that has been deceived in love' and even managed to produce some tears. "If only I had known" she kept repeating. This was a pretty grotesque scene coming from her. The one thing that was uppermost in her mind, as was the case for her whole family when marrying him, was the fact that my younger brother was a British citizen; as if we did not know that.

Upon calling her from Belgium, I hinted at the fact that I liked to be on my own from time to time and that it was not necessary for Max to always accompany me whenever I went out for a walk. That seems to have irked him, although I wonder how she must have told him that. So it happened that all of a sudden, it was not possible anymore to come to live at his place. Looking back at it, he saved my life! Even though because of that we ended up not speaking to each other for years. Years later, I could not believe my luck, when I learned it was possible to go to London on a one-day ticket from Belgium. At least, I thought, I would no longer have to try to entertain someone with whom I never felt comfortable or had nothing in common with. It is not just because of him. Except football, I never really knew what to talk about with Africans, neither did I ever found their stories the most exciting. Try to explain to an

African that is possible to be passionate about reggae music but also enjoy classical music and be a big fan of the Smiths, Muse or Radiohead and see what happens. It has taken me a long time to admit that I never really found myself attracted to Africans in general. When I came on a weekend to London, on Sunday, to please this lump of fat, I accompanied them to one of these so called 'black churches' (meaning evangelical churches) that seem to crop up wherever there are a lot of Africans around. It would be quite a scene in there! I didn't meet any real Brits; be they white or black Britons. It was filled with only Africans, some of them barely speaking any English at all. Like in every self-respecting 'black church,' there would be the obligatory pathetic scene in which some women would fall to the ground in ecstasy. Obviously, this could also have something to do with some more down to earth matters like, perhaps, a legal permission to stay that had recently been granted or a rise in social benefits. None of these people seemed really integrated into British society, even those who might have had a regular job. Any talk related to British culture be it stand-up comedians, TV series must have sounded strangely to them. Actually, I do not even know whether Max knows anything about these stand-up comedians of the likes of Alan Carr, Lenny Henry, Ricky Gervais or Gina Yashere.

The lack of any anything exciting, original stories is the one thing that always strikes me about most Africans, and this applies as well to blacks born or raised in Europe. When this miraculously happens they need to make a movie about it, like '*Etoile Première*' a movie about a black family away on a skiing holiday. One day, I was reading an article about a Belgian football team of the first league (Beveren) in Time Magazine. It is was a team almost entirely made up of Africans that apparently got so famous that even Time Magazine found it worth to dedicate an article to it. In it, one of the few white lads on the team was asked how he got on with his team mates.

"Very well," he said, but what struck him most was the way the Africans seem to handle boredom. "It does not seem to affect them," he added. Bruno and I laughed when we read this. His observation was spot on. Rarely does anyone see an African doing something more creative than playing football, maybe sometimes tennis, but all in all, simple things; things that do not stretch his imagination or may sound too new to him. Do not ask him, for example, if he would be interested in going kayaking or horse riding, as this kind of activities would sound a bit strange to him. It is still relatively new, and this has been going on for only a few years now, seeing groups of black people taking the train to go the coast for a nice day out during the summer. At first, except for those who lived there (usually political refugees), whenever I met one out there it was practically always a black lad amongst a group of white people or a mixed couple (I don't think it was the black person who got the idea to go there first). That is how fun and exciting we are, despite our easy laughs. Of all races, Africans must be the most boring, hollow people on earth; well, certainly for me anyway. Do I care about all this childish excitement in the Congolese diaspora about yet another new *"pas de danse"* that gets much talked about and that everyone wants to try out, as if there was nothing more in life.

In 2008, when I saw a black family renting a go-kart to ride along the promenade with at the coast of Ostend, I could not believe my eyes. It struck me so much that if I had the chance I would probably have taken a picture. Within my black family, most still have never been to the coast. Life in African families seems steeped in boredom from day one. They never seem to know anything as long it is not related to the African community or their Christian evangelical church. Bruno once suggested to some of his black friends to rent a chalet for a few days in Durbuy in the Ardennes, known for its outdoor activities like kayaking, quad, horse riding et cetera. They looked at him as if he had turned mad. I never heard of African parents doing something original with their kids. The concept of family life in African families is totally different compared to what most people know, and it is not always a question of money as most people would like to believe. Except for going to church together, organized family outings like going to a swimming pool, leisure parks or going on a holiday are practically non-existent.

That is why, all in all, I am quite glad to have been abandoned and thankful for the legacy of my white parents more precisely, their way of life. Whatever happened afterwards I had a fantastic family life when growing up. I still have fond memories of the times we went to the coast with our bikes attached to the roof of the car, or we went wandering on rocks at the beach to pick up some mussels which my mother would prepare with French fries; the favourite dish of the Belgians. I always enjoyed hearing this strange West Flemish dialect of the people living there. It is probably the most estranged dialect of the Flemish language. First, we used to go to a holiday resort called "De Duinse Polders" in Blankenberg which incredibly still exist, and afterwards, to Middelkerke where we rented a house. We went there practically every school holiday. It is still one of the most beautiful moments of my life. We played tennis, went to every kind of events that was around, and even hired a little plane once. Come to think of it, it is sometimes difficult to believe that there was ever a time we had several months full of nice weather. Everywhere we went, we were practically always the only blacks. Even as a teenager, it was not by far as cosmopolitan as it is nowadays. This may sound incredible for some people - yet it was! In those days, no one heard about 'political' or 'economic refugees.' Back then, people from foreign backgrounds were barely seen. During the winter when Bruno and I went to Ostend with our bikes, the only blacks we saw were those who played in the basketball team of Ostend. They could easily be recognized because of their height.

For a close friend of mine, a white guy who lived with an African woman, it had always been a struggle for him to interest her in something as simple as going to a park with their kid. Popping out kids as a way of life with all the social benefits attached to it had never been a problem for her with her former African husband, but now having to do something more than just that seemed to bewilder her every time. White people like to say that blacks procreate like animals. Well, I am afraid that they may have a point by saying this. Actually, this could even be a typical black thing: procreating like animals without wanting to be too involved in the children's upbringing. It is certainly more widespread amongst blacks than any other race. The only thing is that talking about animals can only be used as a metaphor of course, because some animals pay more attention to their offspring than some humans do. When someone like Bill Cosby, the famous Afro- American stand-up comedian, dared to criticize these women with three, four kids from different fathers, he got slated for being snobbish or, in other words, for not judging this as normal. I do not want to be judgemental but take that laying hen of a biological mother of mine, for instance. Even though I am quite glad to have been abandoned, I am still entitled to ask myself how this woman - although she is probably not the only one to be blamed in this considering the fact that Africans or black fathers in general are the worse there is - could eat, sleep, go about her daily life, let alone get back on that plane knowing there were still two babies left in the nursing home and growing up in this country. What kind of super whore could she be? I never received the slightest explanation as to how Bruno and I came to be abandoned; neither from Max who has always been close to her, nor from the family. Every time I asked them, they seemed to want to avoid the subject and tended to put the blame on my father. All I know is that it was quite unique at the time because it had never happened before. Ever since this "reunion" came up, she always knew where she could find us but Bruno and I never received so much as a phone call from her. She does not need to bother though because I never gave a shit about her either. Now that she must be old and repulsive and probably reeking of piss as does so many older women due to urine loss, I am even less interested in ever wanting to see her. My real mother, the white one, died a long time ago.

Yet things might have been so different nowadays had she known about all the advantages that befall women here in Belgium and witness how some African women managed to milk and exploit the system to its bone. I am sure that this would probably have made her think twice before abandoning me. Some of these women, Africans and from other foreign backgrounds alike, do sometimes not believe their luck when they compare all their rights and advantages to those of men. Some of these advantages or so call rights are avidly talked about in some communities especially to newcomers in this country. It is generally known that out of fear, people from foreign backgrounds do not want to take a bride any more from their home countries knowing damn well how some of them seem to change abruptly once they are here; having their mouths full of their rights and just cannot shut up any more. The divorce rate is rife among such couples. I could tell the most disgusting stories of abuse about some of these women. On the other hand, I have to admit that it is just fascinating to see how, despite looking so naïve, they know how to milk the system to its bone. Some of them know more about the benefit system than people who have been living here for decades. Nevertheless, this will never be highlighted anyway because in this modern society women are still considered victims and vulnerable creatures, and that is the way they want to keep it. To be cynical about it or put this into doubt would be deemed 'sexist.' The word the western media in general is trying to laden with the same drama and intensity nowadays as the word 'anti-Semite.' I mean, whenever those words gets dropped, expecting to see cars crashing into one and other, people gasping for air or hyperventilating, chandeliers falling from the ceiling, and so forth. Nowadays, there is pure hate within some African and Arab communities about the way some women want to emulate white women by wanting to be independent whenever it suits them and calling the cops at the slightest conflict. This is a call cops seem all too willing to heed in order to save these women from the hands of men from such barbaric cultures. After all the moral superiority of the Belgians has been proven long time ago: same-sex marriages, the fact that gays and lesbians are allowed to adopt children, their legions of pedo-tourists, the list goes on. They are so convinced of the superiority of their moral values that anyone who does not agree with them is either retarded or a fascist. On the other hand, they will never realise the full extent of tricks we, foreigners, play on them. Even if we do not enjoy all the perks that women derived from their status as victims, we certainly know how to sometimes profit from those perks, too. For instance, a Muslim man having his wife tell the authorities that she has been pressurized into wearing a veil or been beaten so that she would be entitled to a whole network of social organisations, with as icing on the cake: a social apartment. Later, she would pretend to be reconciled with her husband - love is full of mysteries - and there you go: both are entitled to the same social apartment! It may be *haram* (against Islam) as one Moroccan friend told me but certainly efficient! An African friend told me that while he was living in a detention centre for refugees here in Belgium, waiting to be granted political asylum and be allowed to leave the place, there was a Congolese guy who pretended to have fled the country for being persecuted because of his sexual orientation. He once said to the social worker in charge of his dossier:

"And if you do not believe me, you may even look at my arsehole." It worked. He got granted asylum and was allowed to leave the detention centre. Now, word got around and all of sudden most African started to use the same claim. Whether they all added that most convincing bit ". . . if you do not believe me you may even look. . ." is still unclear. Some of them must still rue the day they ever mentioned this. For the gay pride parade of 2012 there was a theme about sexual discrimination in Africa and those Africans who claimed to have been discriminated against for their sexual orientation had been asked to participate in the parade. A black British woman living in Belgium, herself a lesbian and a disgusting woman to look at (she looked like the lead singer of Sunk Anansie minus the man-eating fierce expression of her) told me, that some of them were so ashamed they did not know where to hide themselves and that some of them even tried to hide behind the rainbow flag whilst walking in the parade. Welcome to Belgium and its superior moral values! For Arabs another trick that worked quite well for a while in order to be granted political asylum was pretending to be persecuted for having switched to the Christian faith. I never came to know how they had managed to convince all persons concerned with their cases. Did some of them resort to eating bacon in front of their social worker, wear crucifixes, citing psalms from the bible? Stupid Belgians!

For most black women in Belgium the ideal man must be, of course, white. They are 'le pigeon idéal' ('the ideal clown') as they say. They damn well know how kind he is, and how easy they can manipulate him. Some even go as far as to pretend that they prefer white men for being more romantic. Based on what a white friend told me quite proudly of himself is that what African women seem to miss most with black men would be this tongue-kissing. If true this must be the most desperate and grotesque claim I ever heard knowing that sloppy kissing is even rare among young black people who were born and raised in this country. Some even find it pretty disgusting. People tend to forget that it is not essentially a worldwide practice. As if the way white people express their love and affection to each other or "fall in love" would be the only truly way. Even young black girls who are constantly talking about their boyfriends, holding hands like 'couples in love' do, or seen smoking, is still considered as wanting to play white. Besides, women who smoke are still frowned upon in the African community and considered whores. The Belgians cannot have it both ways. For me, personally, one of the most heart-rending scenes I ever witness is still seeing an African woman playing 'the one in love' in the company of a white man. I am especially alluding to women who never had any previous interaction with white people. What makes it all the more heart-rending is knowing that African women are the least refined creatures of all. Even among the younger ones, it is still not surprising to see an African woman walking down the street with such an air about herself that is almost intimidating, only to see her the next minute spit on the ground. They are probably the only ones to do that; well, in Belgium anyway. In Congo, Bruno witnessed something even better. Some people had organised a party to which he was invited. Whilst he sat on the terrace with friends, he saw a woman getting out of a car all dressed-up also going to this party, with such an air about herself as if she was walking down a catwalk. On her way to the place, he saw her all of sudden kneel down to take a leak in the open barely bothering to hide herself from all the people who were sitting outside on the terrace. But what shocked him most was that she just needed to do a few more steps to go inside for the toilets.

One day, Bruno went to visit with his wife and kids the botanic garden of Kisantu. It's a botanic garden created by a passionate Belgian priest who had taken it upon himself to catalogue each plant and make it such a beautiful place as it has become now. It is needless to say that such an initiative would never have been undertaken by an African. Such work would have involved too much patience, organization and, last but not least, refinement. Those kinds of characteristics most Africans are still totally devoid off. He was a bit surprise seeing so many dressed up Congolese coming from church going to such a place; they probably wanted to play "family outing" like they must have seen on TV. At some point, he saw two women looking for a place to take a leak. Well, despite showing them where to go for the toilets and there having no queue or whatsoever around the bathroom, they still preferred to hide themselves between the bushes to take a leak with one woman standing on the lookout. That's how refined these women are. Africans are in manners and behavior the least refined people on earth.

"After a while there," Bruno said with his usual calm, "nothing surprises you anymore."

The Congolese diaspora in Belgium is not really a place in which a person would find solace or help. The hate among countrymen is both legendary and tragic at the same time. The way we gloat in each other's misery and try to look down on one another is well-known and quite unique. When I read a book by Colette Braeckman in which she describes all this bragging, haughtiness and disdain going on within the Congolese diaspora in Belgium, I felt ashamed; but what irked me most was how accurate her description was and the fact she seemed to know too much about us. I have never ceased to be the subject of criticism from my own black family for the way I look. To them, this guy with his dreadlocks can only be a drug addict, a low-life. This could also partly be explained by the natural backwardness of Congolese, or maybe of Africans in general, and the fact that we are extremely superficial. During the summer, it is still not surprising to see Congolese parade themselves on the terraces at 'La Porte de Namur' (a posh area in Brussels), proud they can afford something to eat while hoping that everyone would see them.

We are even laughed at, and with reason, by other Africans because of our constant urge to show off and constant bragging. It is still quite common to encounter a Congolese going about all dressed up, with an air of such self-importance that is almost intimidating yet having no job at all and a future as bleak as mine, trying to make everyone to believe he is the most important person in the world. Some of them, especially older people, still seems to have tribal preoccupations on their minds. Despite being surrounded by all these modern trappings, it is still not rare during a conversation to be asked by an older person from which tribe you are actually part of. I will never feel much empathy for a Congolese who might be going through a rough patch, or any African for that matter. Why should I? We just do not like each other anyway. Despite everything, I would rather help out an Arab. My Moroccan friends are the most reliable friends I can think of. Their reliability is quite unique and maybe is it just an Arab thing. Some Congolese refuse to believe I might actually be one of them as long I do not show them my identity card, which has never disturbed me because I never cared about the Congolese community to start with. It actually flatters me, as if I was supposed to derive some pride from it. This is especially due to my dreadlocks and my morphology. I am very small. Most blacks think I am Senegalese. Getting rid of my Congolese citizenship and finally being granted Belgian nationality was like getting rid of a curse. It had only been a source of misery from day one, especially for anything I had in mind like travelling around the world. With a Congolese passport, this would have been just near impossible. Most countries like France and the Netherlands have always granted double citizenship to those from their present or former colonies as a rule. This had been the case for decades. Not in Belgium. Nowadays to apply for Belgian citizenship has turn into surreal farce. Even someone who has been living illegally in this country and can prove that he was at least five years on Belgian soil can apply for Belgian citizenship and get it in less than two years. I think that such a thing is even unique in the world. I knew a Nigerian who spoke neither French nor Flemish turn a Belgian national just because his children were born here and because he could prove that he lived five years in Belgium. A propos, if a white person would have made the same kind of observations, he would have been immediately branded a racist, as always. Things couldn't' be more different in the nighties. In my case, the procedures to get my Belgian citizenship lasted more than four years and was littered with so many hurdles that I thought I would never see the end of it. This was meant to discourage people from seeking Belgian nationality. The most depressing thing was having to go to the Congolese Embassy for whatever document. I always hated to go there. I was there once with my social assistant when there was apparently some confusion about whose turn it was. A very civilised fat mama pig started to shout at us for no reason at all. Judging by her behaviour, I do not think she missed Africa that much; not while being in this embassy anyway. She probably received the right to work there for being of the same tribe or region of Mobutu, who knows. This embassy supposed to protect us and give us a helping hand has never had any meaning for us, Congolese. I never heard anyone speak positively about it. The Congolese embassy is just a mirror of what my country most resemble like: a banana republic.

Chapter 9

Tintin in Congo

I went to the Congo for the first time in 2009. This mad country of televangelists, crazed warlords, greedy politicians and black magic. A country where a singer like Werrason or some pastors can hold as much sway as the President, which was a factor he could not neglect because of the votes it could bring him during election time. Time will tell whether President Joseph Kabila seems to be part of this dying breed called 'President for life.' With so few credible leaders in the opposition why not try to be one? One serious candidate during the elections of 2011 was Etienne Tshisekedi, a pathetic old man of 200 years old who looked permanently angry because of the fact people had dared to wake him up without announcing him first that, at last, he would be president. One other credible leader of the opposition, at one the time, was Jean-Pierre Bemba alias *"The Chairman"* who had been rumoured (accusations that were proven to be correct) to be the head of an army made up of cannibals with a fondness for pygmy meat as *'plat du jour.'* Even if this utter brutish man alias *"The Chairman"* might not have been present while his soldiers were lying those corpses on the barbecue pit, he should have known that being associated with such barbaric acts would have him sent straight to the international criminal court in The Hague. Though, in order to shed their image of a neo-colonial institution by appointing Fatou Bensouda as Deputy Prosecutor, the only reason of being of the ICC is to judge African leaders. This is common knowledge among Africans. Poor Jean-Pierre, life can be so unfair for us Africans! Maybe he should have used more modern methods to bring mayhem and murder upon a country like did Tony Blair (also called 'The Peace Envoy') with Irak.

Upon arriving at the airport, I stood in the queue for the VIP people. Someone who had been waiting me I had notified the officer

133

at the check point that I was the brother of one of the directors at Malta Forrest and took me out of the queue. Bruno was waiting outside. This caused some amazement among all the self-important dressed-up Congolese because I was just in baggy shorts and trainers. Although I had travelled all over the world and had been warned about some of things I was going to witness, nothing could have prepared me for what I saw at the luggage carousel. The noise and the sight of the officer standing on the carousel waving his baton trying to keep order and threatening to beat anyone who dared to step onto the carousel to retrieve their belongings had straightaway a sobering effect on me. This was just the beginning though. The whole trip to Bruno's apartment of my brother was arduous. We got stuck in the traffic jam, street-lights did not work and everywhere it was crowded. His apartment was situated on the 'Boulevard du 30 Juin' near the headquarters of the Monuc. This hated organisation had done nothing in protecting the people whenever their intervention was needed; everyone was longing to see them leave. The avenue is basically still the only street left in a decent state of repair in the whole of the city, probably even the country. From his window or his balcony, I could see across to the other side of the river, Congo-Brazzaville. My brother had a maid and chauffeur at his disposal. The following day, the latter drove me around the city but his main preoccupation seemed to show me the local beauties. I hated how whenever he presented me to some chicks, he would always specify I was '*un mundélé*' (a white guy) or a bounty (like those sweets black outside but white inside) since it was the first time that I had come back to my motherland and, on top of that, could not even speak Lingala. Women took the mick out of me; they just could not understand that I could not speak one word of Lingala. It hurt me because it reminded me what I always have been and probably always will be: a rootless bastard freak.

On the other hand, I never really understood all this profound talk from people speaking profusely about their African roots because I have never really cared about my African roots in the first place. I had seen enough documentaries about idealistic black

Americans following the lead of Marcus Garvey of going "back to Africa" only to find themselves totally disconnected with the people they called their "brothers" and being laughed at behind their backs. Besides, I wonder sometimes what on earth a black American or someone who has been born or raised in more refined settings than Africa, might have in common with these people. I realised a long time ago that I might have more in common with an Asian, an Indian, or a white person, than with any Africans around here, including some Africans who were born and raised in Europe. While I was there, I have to admit that I tried to play the real African, to blend in somehow, but my attempts were totally ridiculed when talking with an older white man who approached me on the street. I was wearing a typical African dress and oh God did I feel proud that day and so authentic. Now you are a real Congolese! My sister in law told me. I had barely exchanged a few words with this old man when he asked me: "C'est *la première fois que vous venez au Congo?*" (Is it the first time you come to Congo?) I lost any illusion in even trying to pretend again.

Anyway, I feel rather blessed to have left this continent and not to have my fate decided upon by an African government. It is the worst thing that could happen to anyone; in some cases it even amounts to a death sentence unless, that is, the person is from the same tribe of those in power. Yet, ironically, all these African heads of state are asking us to be proud to be African. Some former president of the likes of Idi Amin, Jean-Bedel Bokassa, Mobutu,... could not even keep up any pretence at civilisation: they came straight out of the bushes

I must admit Bruno was right when he told me I might be surprised once I saw the women there, knowing my overwhelming dislike of African women. Indeed, I am not saying that I found them all of a sudden so gorgeous but the fact is that some of them really were. I know this sound terribly cliché but it is because I had never paid the slightest attention to them and, being there, I had somehow no other option than to do so. The following days, I even went a bit further than just looking at them. Another aspect I found quite

135

exciting during my stay there was that no one could ever accuse me of being a sexual tourist: I was in my own country for God's sake! I had almost forgotten about that. I was allowed to indulge in it as much as I wanted to without any moral strings attached. Not that I found these women much worth it. Whatever their reputation for being so hot, African women must be the most boring creatures in bed. Some sexual practices that are considered ordinary in most parts of the world are looked at with disgust there. No matter how much money I was prepared to give them, they just did not want to hear of oral sex. All over the world black men are obsessed by curvy round butts, which might be my only true African heritage. Some black women have got such so voluminous butts that they pose a threat to the ozone-layer. Yet when it comes down to big arses I am as African as you can be. Well, in Congo, just like anywhere else where people are more obsessed with butts as opposed to breasts like in the west, women would do anything to catch your attention by wearing thigh things; but do not try to have anything more in mind with their butts during sex there. To be honest, I already knew about that. In Belgium, a black cousin once told me that for such things I would probably have to cross the whole of Congo before meeting an African woman who would be willing to do that. In Belgium, a former close friend of mine, a Flemish guy, pathologically obsessed by African women told me how frustrating his relations were in bed. He had to discuss and beg for everything. Some of the African women he dated found even tong-kissing so awful that they would brush their teeth immediately afterwards. How romantic! He also once told me that most women from Nigeria he slept with had their clitoris excised, which did not seem to bother them at all as they found this practice a perfectly normal operation. They said that it make them feel "clean". Well, I 'm not going to sympathise with the frustrations of this Flemish guy. This disgusting human being was HIV positive yet he never warned any of his conquest about it or bothered to use a condom. I guess maybe because they were *just* African women he felt allowed to do that.

136

Yet some of the things African women are so fiercely opposed to would be a nice cheap way to combat this demographic explosion taking place in Congo like on the rest of the black continent. It is still a big thing in Congo, even for the more sophisticated families, to have many children. Every Congolese family has an average of five kids.

My chauffeur, for example, had six kids. Most men who worked for Bruno there had a minimum of five kids. How they were going to feed them or pay for their studies is the least of their concerns for an African contrary as you would expect from more *refined* people.

Anyway, except for '*les beautés locales,*' I am afraid there is not that much to see in Kinshasa. Yet I started to better understand why some expats and work colleagues of Bruno used to shorten their holidays whilst in Europe to get back in Congo. I am talking especially about the white menfolk. Here they stay young, can get all the girls they want and get rich along the way. Who would not envy them, as a man? Like in most black African countries, white people are still treated with far more consideration than blacks do with their own people. You still see blacks cowering in front of white people. On my first day, I got involved in a heavy argument at a cafeteria of a posh tennis club frequented by expats. While I was sitting with Bruno and a friend of his, a black waiter asked us if we did not want to sit at another place which was less comfortable when he saw white people looking for a place to sit. I just lost it and started to call him all kind of names in front of everyone, telling him that he was a sad Negro and that it was because of people like him that we were still lagging behind. In turn, he said that I was a bandit and that he could see it because of my dreadlocks.

"Mal élevé!" (ill-mannered) he kept saying with his strong African accent. It was not Bruno's first stay in Congo before he found work there. He had already been there during the wedding of my younger brother Max, the one from London. It was the first time he met our biological mother. She had come down all the way from Angola for this event. They barely spoke to each other and neither did she ask after me. This must have been a proud mum, after all. Her eldest

137

daughter she had not seen in decades living in Brazil, another of her daughters was a whore - a trait that seems to run in the family - and a son she had still never seen. I wonder what must be the mental state of such a woman. She was by all accounts a very refined woman. She seemed to have no sense at all of what the main course for dinner was, so she just put everything on one plate. It amazed me for I thought she was part - or at least had been part - of those more 'refined' well off people.

Being made redundant after the collapse of the Telecom sector in Belgium and after again being discriminated against during the following years by every single construction company, Bruno finally got the chance to work as a construction engineer with the status of an expatriate in Congo. There was a shortage of construction engineers, and the fact he was black and had been raised and educated in Belgium was an added bonus for the company he was going to work for.

"Do not take it too personally," they told him during his job interview at the headquarters in Wavre, "you will better understand once you are there." He did not really need to; he knew how we are. Yet, he too came to be taken aback by some of the things he was going to witness. I will never forget what he once said during his leave in Belgium; it was all the more shocking for the fact that he had always been so pro-black unlike me. I am sure white people would have liked to hear it, which is why I prefer not to repeat it. Besides, if a white person would have said exactly the same thing he told me about the Congolese, it would have been branded as racist; as always. Basically what it comes down to is that, because of our mentality, this country could and will never ever evolve. Well, certainly not at the pace progress is judged by. He started as an engineer and worked his way up to become one of the directors at Malta Forrest, earning money he would never have been able to make in Belgium. He must have laughed at his luck! He was at the head of some construction projects - most of them financed with Chinese money - so big that just to look at them was enough to give you a headache. Like, for instance, the haven of Mbandaka, one of *'les 5 chantiers'* ('the 5

138

worksites') which President Kabila intended to showcase to the people before the elections came up. I wonder whether therein laid not the President's unique ambition: have something to brag about and showcase to the people. What a great man! Rarely has an African leader shown any ambition in developing his country. Actually, it would be totally at odds with the mind-set of most African leaders as well as for those coming to power regarding their application of one of their most famous sacred principle: "Now it is our time to eat!" So why should he be any different? There is nothing left in this country from of what was basically already a pile of rubble! Walking around the city, except for the mansions built by the nouveau rich and parvenus and some nice apartment blocks of Lebanese owners, there are not any eye-catching nice buildings to look at; everything seems in a derelict state. This place is worse off than during the reign of Mobutu but this not the fault of President Kabila. The only thing is that Mobutu managed to hold on a little longer to what the Belgians left us. There is barely a proper infrastructure to speak of as you would be expecting in this day and age. Congo, like so many other parts on the black continent, is a shameful place. A symbol for what black Africa stands for; an utter failure! It does not seem to matter how rich an African country may be in resources or the amount of money you put into the hands of those African leaders, the result has and will always be the same: misery, upon misery. Traditionally in such countries, the only road to be in a good state would be the one that leads from the airport to the centre of town as I had expected when coming here. Well, this being Congo, it was not even the case.

It is sometimes difficult to believe that, despite all the atrocities the Belgians committed in my country, they left us a country that was one of the most advanced and modern on the black African continent. Anyone just has to look at these old pictures or documentaries to be reminded of that. I have no doubts that with the passing of time all of this material will gain even more in value; probably even become collectors' items as it already might be the case. Truth be told, their comfort was paramount to the Belgians and to achieve it and be better placed to suck the country dry of its resources, the Belgians were forced to build all types of infrastructure.

The former French president Nicolas Sarkozy was partly right in his controversial speech during a visit to Senegal when he said that the problem of the African was that he still had not fully entered history yet. I said 'partly' because the French president should have been more precise and say that it is the African's proper history that seems to always catch up with him. If nowadays you do not say something lyrical about Africa as an African, people say "*Il est complexé*" (he has got an inferiority complex) and, in case of a white person, "that he is prejudiced." I am sure that most Africans still thank God that Nicolas Sarkozy did not make his speech in front of the preposterous museum of "black civilisations" which was still in construction at the time. It would have made the whole event sound even crueller. His speech shocked many Africans around the world. White women would learn a lot from Africans on how to put on a shocked face. Due to our culture of victimisation it is, with dancing, one of the few things we have become expert at. It is a fact that only a handful of African countries had been able to handle the modern infrastructure inherited from their former colonial masters. Most African countries relapsed ineluctably into their former primitive state once they gained their independence.

Maybe it would not be such a bad idea to see our former colonial masters hand out a sort of '*Carte d'Immatriculation*' (registration card) again like those that were first issued in 1952 by the Belgian colonial authorities to Congolese who had reached the status of "*évolué*" (enlightened). Congolese were entitled to this status through a registration card if they could prove that they were impregnated by western culture and had been fully assimilated by "Belgian ideals and way of life." A social assistant would come over to your home and verify whether the interior of your home had a sofa, a couch, whether your family ate with fork and knives, how your shoes looked like and so forth. On top of that, the men had also to prove they had renounced entirely polygamy and witchcraft. These registration cards were only handed out to men but it was the whole family who

140

benefited from it. At the time, these cards meant a lot to Congolese people because it was seen as a step up the social ladder; many also thought (falsely) that this would entitle them to the same privileges of the whites. These cards were hard to get by; it is estimated that from 1952 to 1959 only 250 of these registration cards were delivered to *"évolués"*. Some of the winners of those cards were shown on TV as examples and sources of inspiration. The man of the house was filmed reading the newspaper in front of the TV while the children were doing their homework and his wife (only one wife!) domestic chores; playing out domestic life as in any "civilised" (white) family household. The most famous person to have ever received such a card was Patrice Lumumba. Obviously, these cards would have a different meaning now and be totally devoid of its racist ideology. It would be adapted to these times - political correctness oblige - but the spirit, that of enlightenment, should remain the same. This time, however, they would be issued to any African statesmen who managed to muster enough courage to think beyond the well-being of his own tribe - an almost impossible task for most of them - have the ambition to develop his country and invest in education and other social actions. I am afraid this will always remain just what it is: wishful thinking.

Everyone who has just a little knowledge of the mind-set of Congolese or Africans in general knows that we are a doomed people carrying the seeds of our own tragedy. We are foremost the victims of the way we are and the politicians, as any politicians would do, are just tapping into what we inherently are: the most corrupt, farcical, buffoonish people on earth! Some Belgian politicians too should bear the blame for this starting with the greatest buffoon of them all Louis Michel *'L'ami des Africains'* ('The friend of Africans') and head of the francophone MR political party. He do not seem to realise it but he is a laughing stock among the Congolese people. This sad clown is also a great admirer of Leopold II and does not understand why people should keep focusing on his misdeeds.

"This man" (referring to Leopold II) as he once said, "had just great ideas for such a little country as Belgium." Belgian politicians seem always to have been complementing our African leaders in the spirit of the "Noble Savage' for going backward - at least that way, they stay closer to nature they must have thought - instead of going forward. Indeed, the more they saw this country going down the drain, the more they seemed to praise our leaders. One Flemish minister, Karel De Gucht, did not seem at all that charmed by this ideal of the 'Noble savage' and, as any normal person would do, he asked a few legitimate and more contemporary questions to President Joseph Kabila.

"What have you done concretely since you took charge?" He asked. "How do you explain this rampant misery, degradation, corruption all around you?" It caused a massive diplomatic row, as was to be expected, and for a while he had been refused entry to the country as persona non grata. Remarkably, he even got criticized by Walloon politicians for having been too brutal. Among other things, they accused him of behaviour that was reminiscent of the worst days of Belgian colonialism. The truth is that President Joseph Kabila is not better or worse than the rest of them. He is just an African leader with everything what this entails. Having said that, of all the buffoons who wanted to be president I think that President Kabila is the most suited person to get this country ahead. Yet it is a mystery to me how the president could show himself so sensitive to what Karel de Gucht said. Does he not know that he is overseeing a country which finds itself at the bottom on the list of countries with the lowest Human Development Index in the world? That they are students attending computer classes without any computers around? The education system in Congo has turn into a hopeless farce that goes beyond words.

Wandering around Kinshasa, I wondered if there could be any rational explanation for this total collapse in infrastructure and perennial failure at modernisation concerning most African countries. I was struck by a comment made by a young lady at a barbecue there about the old houses found in Belgium which she was hoping to be able to see one day. On her first visit to Belgium, Bruno's wife, an

African woman, was also charmed about the old houses she came across in Belgium. At that time, it had not really sunk in yet; I could not understand why they would be so fascinated about all these old houses. What is so exciting about old houses, anyway? Does every civilisation not have them? Now by walking around this derelict city of Kinshasa, certain things started to gradually dawn on me. I wondered:

"Where were we only one century ago? Could it be that we were still living in the bushes?" Come to think of it, I am afraid this might not just be a rhetorical question. It is an embarrassing truth to have to admit that before the first white priests came to Congo, there was absolute nothing. There are no old houses, let alone big constructions to speak of, pre-dating colonisation in Congo. It is not like they had ever been destroyed by an earthquake, as far as I know. Also, I do not think that on the black continent there were ancient medieval cities on the scale of Nuremberg or Dresden before they got criminally erased from the map by allied bombing during the second war, or typical houses like in Sana'a (Yemen) dating back from in the middle-ages. Of all races, Africans are the only ones who haven't built anything on a grand scale and have intellectually contributed the least to civilisation. Actually 'the least' might even be a euphemism because I really do not know what our precise intellectual legacy to civilisation actually might be.

There are bound to have been African empires as anyone would expect on an African continent. So what? I never understood all this zeal from some African writers to constantly remind us of that so that we could also revel in a glorious past. I found it quite depressing when Sylvia Serbin, the writer of the book Queens of Africa, told on TV that when she talked to Africans students about some great African empires, some of them started to cry. I did not know that our inferiority complex ran so deep. But which are my cultural links with the descendants of the empire of Dahomey in Benin, for example? Or do I have to revel in their glorious past just because they also happened to be black. How absurd is that! Yet there is still a difference between civilisation and empires. For me a civilisation is something that includes an intellectual legacy to the world, something that inspired intellectually and eventually helped to give birth to another civilisation. That is why I cannot understand how anyone can have the guts to speak about a black civilisation in the absence of any written language. The much acclaimed BBC 'Lost Kingdoms of Africa' documentary had been for me more a desperate attempt at trying to give us something we never had: a proper civilisation. I quit watching the documentary after the first instalment. Maybe they should have broadcast it to the people that were seen arriving on *pateras* in Spain (Spanish for little boats) or Lampedusa in Italy trying to flee the 'Kingdom of Africa' while having as background music the song 'Exodus' of Bob Marley.

Some of the most known Afro-centrists like Cheikh Anta Diop or Asanté Molefi Kete seemed to be running wild by their crushing inferiority complex. Anyone just has to read their absurd views in which they claim that every great culture can be traced back to African roots and that the Egyptians were actually blacks and thus built the pyramids. If indeed we really built them, it did not seem to have been much of an inspiration to other black African countries. The yearly 'Black History Month' that takes place in the United States as well in Britain may be a nice attempt at boosting the self-esteem of black people in highlighting and commemorating the achievements of some black inventors, scientists and other great personalities in any specific field to the general public. Yet most of those claims have been proven to be false. Besides, this kind of knowledge never help me to pay my bills to start with. I wonder if during 'Black History Month,' black people ever heard that most blacks were sold as slaves by their own people through black kings and tribal leaders and that it was those kings and tribal leaders who provided the whole infrastructure in order to have it run smoothly. Well, I guess not by reading the book '*Roots*' by Arthur Haley. If the author is accurate Africa was almost a paradise-like place before the white man set foot on the black continent (there is not much to believe in what he wrote anyway. All his facts turned out to be a complete invention and he has even been accused of plagiarism). Anyway, the whole event lost its significance long time ago by focusing more on black celebrities than ancient African history. I am tired of all this criticism and absurd claims of reparations coming from ignorant blacks directed to whites about our slavery past without ever mentioning the real culprits: the Arabs. What whites and Jewish merchants (Jews played a crucial role in the slave trade, which is often been overlooked) did to us for the transatlantic slave-trade was peanuts in comparison to what Arabs did. Slavery is not just a story about white versus black people; it is a bit more complicated than that. Slavery existed in every society, even among tribes; white people were also enslaved. But it is what Arabs-Muslims specifically did to black people that rank as one the greatest crime against humanity eclipsing by far the genocide of Jews. For some reason these facts have always been occulted for whatever political correct reason. I don't think that Malcolm knew about this too on his trip to Mecca and even if he knew it would have conveniently ignored it. His hate was too great towards the white people, which I can understand after everything he went through.

One day, it would be nice to see a Kunta Kinte movie in the Arab world set this time. Since Kunta Kinte was a Muslim, he should know his way around in any of these Muslims countries and it should be quite easy to find extras, and for free, knowing that slavery still does exists in some Muslim countries like Mauritania, Niger, Saudi-Arabia or Soudan. It is a mystery that no one ever thought about that before considering the low-cost such a production would entail. White people should stop to harbour any guilty feelings about our colonial or our slavery past. We are far more harsh and cruel among ourselves than whites have ever been towards us. It is about time that we blacks face up to this reality and stop using the white man as a scapegoat for everything that goes wrong in Africa. Considering everything that has been going on in black Africa, white people deserve an amnesty for anything bad they did to us. I, for one, would be prepared to declare this officially with ceremony and everything included. Among the guests, I would invite one of my favourite French stand-up comedians and notorious anti-Semite Dieudonné and ask him to take place in the front row so that he would not miss one word about what I have got to say. Dieudonné never ceases to blame whites and Jews alike for all the ills to befall black people, never ceases to remind them what they did to us during slavery but, just like so many people, he seems mute where the Arabs-Muslims are concerned. Irritating coward! As with our colonial past, it is far more fun and simple to discharge all our woes and frustrations on the white man. This is quite ironic, really, knowing that the primary source of misery to affect black people always stemmed from the black man itself. There has never ever been a greater enemy to black people than the black man himself.

During my one week stay in Congo, I played golf and tennis at a hotel and went to visit the bonobo monkeys. They are only to be found in my country. People called them also 'hippie monkeys' as they would rather prefer to 'make love than war'. I wished this could have been the case for my country. However, this wish might carry a boomerang effect given all the relentless sexual abuse and rape that has been taken place in my country. Congo has been considered to be the rape capital of the world by the Human Rights organisation there. Well, I do have my doubts about such a statement as do so many people there. Everyone knows that the Human Rights organisation lives on this issue and that it needs to keep making these big statements in order to get funding. Actually, it is even a disgusting and a hateful statement to make knowing that these barbaric acts occurred in the region of Kivu nearby the border with Rwanda by marauding militias funded by a war criminal and personal friend of Tony Blair, Paul Kagame. The region of Kivu is not the whole of Congo as far as know. It is like saying that every Congolese is a potential rapist. I wonder how western countries would react to such a label. Having a city like Liverpool being overwhelmed by cases of rapes and the next day seeing it label in every foreign newspaper as being 'the rape capital of the world.'

There is no denying that in these war-affected regions it is probably worse than Afghanistan to be a woman. There at least women do not get rape on such a large scale as it has been the case in

146

my country. This country, as is the case with so many other black African countries, has been blighted by unimaginable savagery of the kind probably only found on the black Africa continent; as if we had some patent on that. Yet, whilst 'Weapons of War,' the Dutch documentary about the rape of women in my country was praised everywhere, another documentary 'Gender Against Men' from Chris Dolan about the rape of men which is endemic in black Africa and widely under-reported, got thwarted from all sides. Nobody wanted to get involved in its production and, when by some miracle it got produced, no one wanted to screen it anywhere. NGOs, aid agencies and the UN still do not recognise the rape of men as a crime. For the simple reason that international bodies still persist to see women as the 'good guys' and men as the 'bad guys.' There is still not even a legal framework to address these issues. This is quite strange considering the west obsession with gay rights in Africa as if we had no more pressing matters to deal with.

With the whole family, we also went to a place I thought was like heaven on earth. Well, I certainly did not expect to find it in my country. Actually, it looked quite incongruous even being surrounded by all this misery. It is was a place that resembled a recreational park where people could do all kind of water sports, strangely exclusively pursued by whites, and be served the best fish in the world. We also organized a kind of Congo River trip on Bruno's boat. I do not think that, despite all its rich resources, this country will ever again achieve the level of modernity it once enjoyed, or one day remotely look like South Africa. Bruno went there to celebrate New Year as do so many Congolese who can afford it. South Africa has also been for years been a magnet for Congolese trying to flee poverty at home only to suffer incredible discrimination there. Like anyone, even more so for blacks, who go there for the first time, Bruno was struck by how modern this country looks like. After all, this was an African country. It is by far one of the most modern countries on the black continent and this is by no means a coincidence. It is almost obligatory to talk about apartheid when you go there to show a concern for a better world. Yet there are some things people would never dare to say aloud: Had it not been for the whites, would this country ever have achieved this level of modernity? In what way, except dancing their very refined toyi-toyi dance which consist in jumping from one foot to the other while walking during a protest march - one cannot help to think about all these potholes that must emerge once these big mamas are gone - did Africans contribute to making it so modern? I do not think their intellectual contribution had much influence on the layout of cities, for example. During his stay, he saw on the telly President Zuma, a man supposed to represent all people, in Zulu dress celebrating his fourth marriage and, as always, dancing. Every time I saw this man on the telly, he seemed to be dancing. I often wonder what must be the preoccupation of such a great intellectual regarding road networks, education, infrastructure and other products of modernity. This kind of preoccupations could not have been much more intense than that of his predecessor (Mbeki) who always played down the AIDS problematic in his country and had, in accordance with his minister of health, set up a stand selling garlic in order to combat it. Africa might be the birthplace of humanity but definitely not of its intellect. In South-Africa one can do the most diverse outdoor activities on hand: hiking, shark diving, paragliding, go on safaris, et cetera; activities blacks never care much about even though I am sure they would pretend otherwise. In order to do that, some kind of infrastructure was needed that would not even have existed were it not for the whites. Same can be said for safaris. An African would rather eat these animals if they depended on him or chopped them into pieces to be sold as bush meat. If gorillas in Rwanda or in my country they did not bring in so much money and were not fiercely protected, every single one of them would have been eaten long time ago. It is generally known that Africans do not really understand all this buzz white people have for wildlife but just because they see it brings in a lot of money, they want to have their share of it too. So when it comes to wildlife, they are posing as the most sensitive blokes. Obviously, I am for affirmative action but they are some things one cannot deny are just too grotesque for words.

At a hotel called 'The Memling,' which was one of the few luxury hotels in Kinshasa, I met a childhood friend called Jo. He was head of security there. He was a crook; always had been, and actually quite rather good at it. He is part of a growing number of people I met there that migrated back to the motherland. His ex-wife is a close friend of mine. I met him three years prior at a barbecue she organized but they were already separated by then. I still wonder what could have been the reason for him to drop her. She was the loveliest woman anyone could find and was a damn beauty. The kind of woman that, African woman or not, I would not have hesitated to be with for a while. At that time, she was thirty-five years old. I asked her what on earth she did to look so good despite already having had three kids. Well, I did not say that in those exact words.

"Nothing, what do you want me to do?" she answered. She looked ten years younger than her age as is often the case with so many beautiful black women - and I am talking about the ones born or raised in Europe. This has really nothing to do with this depressing classic story of white girls telling everyone that when they go shopping with their mothers, people actually think that they are sisters! Followed by their even more depressing giggling. How sad! I am so glad to be born a man. When she asked me to wait a bit until I met her sister, who was already forty but looked even younger than her, she was right. I do not think you see that among white women. They always seem to age before their time, maybe thanks to their lovely symbol of freedom: the cigarette. Anyway, I would be surprised should I ever go back to Congo again. For some reason I had never shown much interest to go there in the first place. Now that I had seen it, I would not mind never seeing it again. Gosh, do I care about such a country!

I had long been disillusioned about Africa before I even went there. Going there did not help to change my mind about some of the things I saw. Despite its racist portrayal of Africans in 'Tintin in the Congo' (referring to the comic strip) nothing has changed much since we came in contact with the outside world; neither mentally nor intellectually. By far the best documentary that gives a good insight into the psyche of Africans in general must be *'Les Marchands de Miracles'* ('Peddlers in Miracles') which was filmed in my country. It is available for free on the internet. It is about the influence of witchcraft and traditional religion on the daily life of people from all walks of life and regardless of their level of education. It shows how people would rather go to a sorcerer rather than rely on conventional medicines. Much of the focus is placed on the all-powerful pastors. Maybe the most crazy part is when someone who desperately ill, calls for one of the pastors who happens to be in his car, for some healing advice. This was just a minor problem for the pastor; he was a talented man and could do so many things at once so he started to pray for the poor man through the telephone telling him he was all right now and to stop worrying. The documentary also showcased some aspects of these huge mass celebrations where at the sign of a pastor, his followers in a trance-like manner, tried to exorcise the demon by shouting words like "No, devil, I am stronger than you!" and other highbrow stuff. It would be wrong to look at it in a picturesque condescending way, for the truth of the matter is: these people are real savages. Let there be no doubt about it and this is something people had better keep in mind! They do not need much of an impulse to reveal their true colours, and that is the whole embarrassing truth. One bad word about you from the pastor or a rumour that you might be a *kindoki* (evil spirit possess by the devil) that needs to be dealt with and it is game over! There have even been some cases of 'child witches' or 'ritual killings' registered in Belgium, France and England. Apparently, for some people, Africa had never been that far away. In England, they set up a special unit after 'The Torso case' when they found the torso of a child that had been the victim of a ritual killing floating in the River Thames; they never managed to catch the killers. It started to dawn on them that they might be dealing with things they never thought possible before in the modern world. For whatever reason, whenever there is pure savagery at work based on some strange religious-inspired motives, an African always emerges. These acts of pure savagery may as well have a stamp on them: 'Made in Black Africa.' I think I may have a perfect explanation for that: atavism. It does not really matter what we read or how intensely we get educated, we Africans will always fall more easily prey to that kind of crap. It has to do with our roots, psyche and mind-set and it is because of all this depressing bullshit that we have always been lagging behind. That is how much I think about cultural relativism. A cynic might point out that these kinds of things are rather to be expected from people who contributed nothing intellectually to civilisation.

I do not care much whether my country ever gets to rise up again or whether black Africa is too often wrongfully portrayed as a desperate place, as some white (snobbish) people like to claim. They must have been charmed by one of the most advance healthcare systems in the world regarding amputations performed for free by cross-dressing cannibals under the reign of Charles Taylor, the former president of Liberia and one of the most pure savages this world has ever known. Little do I care about this cosmetic change the magazine "the Economist" did by describing Africa as the "hopeful continent" instead of the "hopeless continent" as they had done in the beginning after much complains from Africans and left liberals. For my part, it may have stuck with what it said from the beginning. Anyway, they may try rebrand Africa as much as they want to, what matters is that I got out of there! A joy that also seems to have been shared by the former boxer Mohamed Ali while he was in Africa. "I'm so glad my granddaddy took that boat" he famously said. Africa is still a long way off Ubuntu. I did not see much of that concept during my stay there. One of the most poignant images that stayed with me was that of the officer with his baton standing on the carousel at the airport threatening to beat anyone who dared to step onto it. It did not bother him to show the world the kind of place we had just arrived. The truth is that he had no other options than to act like that. Had he not been there, this place would probably have been stormed as expected from such an "enlightened people" like ours and the repository of such a great civilisation.

Ladies and gentlemen, we have lost and we know it. Judging by the unashamed publicity on big billboards I saw everywhere along the streets in Kinshasa for products to lighten the skin, we seem somehow to be aware that we are a doomed race and that this place is curse. As if surrounded by all this misery and sheer hopelessness, we were trying to find some light into ourselves.

Some people were right all along about Congo, or maybe of Africa in general, and knew all too well from the beginning what its essence was all about: The heart of darkness.